LUCIFER
AND THE HIDDEN
DEMONS

A PRACTICAL GRIMOIRE FROM
THE ORDER
OF UNVEILED FACES

Theodore Rose

TABLE of CONTENTS

The Lucifer Paradigm   9
The Requirement   23
The Pathway   29
The Demonic Source   43
The Magickal State   47
Naming Conventions   51
Perspective on The Demons   55
Summoning Demons   61
An Illustrated Working   75
Your Pathway to The Demons   79

To Manipulate Reality   81
Influence, Compelling, and Controlling   82
Financial Situations   84
Sex, Passion, and Seduction   85
Persuasion, Charm, and Trust   86
Healing and The Body   87
Guidance and Wisdom   88
To Find Peace   89
Legal Problems and Justice   90
Willpower and Personality   91
Protection and Binding   92
Personal Skills and Creativity   93
Corruption and Cursing   94
Causing Disease and Injury   95
For Mental Suffering   96
To Create Illusion   97

The Four Demon Kings   99
Lucifer   101
Leviathan   102
Shahtan   103
Belial   104

The Eight Dukes of Lucifer   105
Astaroth   107
Asmodi   108
Oriens   119
Ariton   110
Magoth   111
Beelzebub   112
Paymon   113
Amaymon   114

The Demon Servants of Oriens, Paymon, Ariton, and Amaymon   115
Moreh   117
Frasis   118
Myrmo   119
Trapis   120
Parelit   121
Obedemah   122
Hasperim   123
Fasma   124
Nogah   125
Ethanim   126
Melabed   127
Apolion   128
Asturel   129
Hagrion   130
Liriol   131
Asorega   132
Ragaras   133
Ilekal   134
Sarasim   135
Sigis   136
Laralos   137
Ipakol   138
Balabos   139
Nolom   140
Amillis   141

The Demon Servants of Astaroth and Asmodi   143
Lagiros   145
Ugalis   146
Dagulez   147
Bialod   148
Ranar   149
Buriub   150
Nimalon   151
Bagalon   152
Anamalon   153
Sagarez   154

The Demon Servants of Asmodi and Magoth   155
Kela   157
Diopes   158
Magyros   159
Lamargos   160
Disolel   161

The Demon Servants of Amaymon and Ariton ... 163
Harog ... 165
Agebol ... 166
Rigolen ... 167
Irasomin ... 168
Elafon ... 169

The Demon Servants of Astaroth ... 171
Iromenis ... 173
Apormanos ... 174
Ombalafa ... 175
Kataron ... 176
Iloson ... 177
Kalotes ... 178
Golog ... 179

The Demon Servants of Asmodi ... 181
Maggid ... 183
Gillamon ... 184
Ybarion ... 185
Bakaron ... 186
Presfees ... 187
Hyla ... 188
Ormion ... 189

The Demon Servants of Oriens ... 191
Gagarin ... 193
Sarsiel ... 194
Sorosoma ... 195
Zagal ... 196
Turitil ... 197

The Demon Servants of Ariton ... 199
Nilion ... 201
Maranaton ... 202
Calamosi ... 203
Rosaran ... 204
Semeot ... 205

The Demon Servants of Magoth   207
Tagora   209
Corocon   210
Dulid   211
Arakison   212
Daglus   213

The Demon Servants of Beelzebub   215
Diralisin   217
Camalon   218
Bilek   219
Corilon   220
Borob   221
Gramon   222

The Demon Servants of Paymon   223
Sumuron   225
Ebaron   226
Zalomes   227
Takaros   228
Zugola   229

The Demon Servants of Amaymon   231
Akorok   233
Dalep   234
Bariol   235
Cargosik   236
Nilima   237

Working with Lucifer   239
Conclusion   241
Further Reading   243

The Lucifer Paradigm

There are forces at work that defy everyday logic. These forces bring power and light to the lives of those who embrace the energies that some call darkness. Others know that all power works through the manipulation of light. There is magick in the world, and for those with courage, magick brings power.

The magick in this book gives you powers that include influence and control, with magick for money, sex, passion, and seduction. There are powers of persuasion, charm, and trust alongside those for healing, guidance, wisdom, and peace. The demons enable you to solve legal problems, finding justice and improving your willpower. You will discover protection, bindings, and ways to improve personal skills and creativity. For those who seek greater control, there is a sequence of corruption and cursing rituals and methods for causing disease and mental suffering. Other powers create illusion or concealment and even manipulate time and reality itself. All such claims are nothing but an empty boast until tested by you.

The Order of The Unveiled Faces has performed magick with the powers of Lucifer and The Hidden Demons for many years. Our work began in 1955. In more contemporary times, for reasons that will be elucidated as this book elaborates the concepts central to the workings, all that we have known to be true has been brought to a shining clarity. It is now, with our new certainty, and experience based on our illumined knowledge, that we are willing to reveal what we know, mindful that our words will fall on many deaf ears.

You will find in these pages, the offices, powers, and methods of summoning for Lucifer and over one hundred demons. For those who dare to unshackle themselves from the fear of change, there is a pathway into magick that can bring you more than we would dare to tell you.

Other lives, such ordinary lives, seek to find an existence of pleasure and passion through belief, custom, and exertion.

Whether they know it or not, such lives are based on the dogma of science, the religion of hard work, and the myth of fair reward. Those who suffer from being ordinary bathe in the medicine of therapy, avoidance, affirmations, and wishful thinking. Striving for an enjoyable and fulfilling life without the powers of magick brings depression, sickness and an overpowering feeling of having gone astray.

Most who seek a better life feel worse for having made the attempt. It is a sad truth that for the average person who cannot accept magick, accepting a meagre destiny is less painful than seeking a better life. Without magick, you are walking with the unfulfilled. With magick, you can move beyond the life you were assigned by the misfortune of circumstance.

You will benefit from this magick if you sense that you have within you more than a little intelligence, a strand of creativity and, it must be said, a rebellious nature. If you only exist to please others, to kneel before the demands of happenstance, and to let fate run its course, the methods revealed here will be anathema to you.

The magick disclosed here requires a sacrifice from you, but a sacrifice so trivial that you will not tremble. This sacrifice is only your time and your willingness to experience the magick no matter what that experience becomes. When you are clear about your desires, there is no risk in surrendering to the magick. You are not selling your soul or making a pact with the Devil, but connecting to a legion of consciousness that rewards desire, choice, and determination.

If you are capable of advancing into magick with the willingness to let it change your life, you will see wonders, and you will be granted the power to shape, guide and transform your reality.

Where there was effort, there will be ease.

Where there was fear, there will be control.

Where there was lack, there will be wealth.

If you fear evil, know that there is no evil in this grimoire, other than the evil that you bring. Power is the power to cause change, and the wise bring about change only when they are at ease with a future designated by design and wisdom. Be at ease with your desires, and you will not falter.

You may be required to let go of preconceived notions. To begin with this unshackling, let us look for a moment at Lucifer. For those with little education in the matter, this word or name is synonymous with the Devil or Satan. I confess that my understanding of the word Lucifer, from early childhood, was that it was a name for the tempting light of a fallen angel.

Lucifer is the ruling Demon King as described in sources such as *The Book of Oberon, The Book of The Office of Spirits*, and *The Magical Treatise of Solomon* (all written between 1400 and 1600), but you may believe Lucifer is a Biblical demon, or even The Devil of the Bible, which is a much older source. This is understandable.

A modicum of research will reveal that the Lucifer of the Bible was derived from a single word in Isiah 14:12. Written in Hebrew that word is Heylel. When that was translated into Latin, it came out as 'lucifer,' which is not a name. It means 'morning star,' and in modern Bibles, translators know this, and use 'morning star' instead of 'lucifer' to avoid confusion.

In popular culture and society, it is widely believed that Lucifer is the Devil, the Antichrist, or Satan. This is because, over many centuries, Christian tradition took that Latin word 'lucifer' and through superstition, twisted it into the name Lucifer and then made that name synonymous with the Devil. In the Bible itself, the word 'lucifer' describes a morning star; a metaphor for a King of Babylon. The word has nothing to do with fallen angels or demons.

Those who believe Lucifer is the Devil or a 'light bearer,' do so because they have clung to a Christian tradition that arose because of some clumsy misunderstanding of Latin.

For the occultist, minimal reading of only a limited number of more ancient grimoires, and perhaps some Gnostic works and Apocrypha, along with Canaanite texts, make it apparent that Lucifer is a Demon King who will come to you when summoned.

If you are captivated by such matters, you can research this, but finding a single truth that will satisfy all analysis is impossible. Finding a truth that leads to workable magick is something we have accomplished. It is clear that Lucifer was known as a demon, a pagan god, and many other forms of spirit, in many cultures long before the Bible was written.

For the working occultist, what matters is that the grimoires of magick that appeared between 1400 and 1600, retained and passed on the pre-Biblical knowledge, which had been hidden for centuries, and gave those who were able to look a glimpse of the true Lucifer and his Legion of Demons. The Lucifer of the Bible can be dismissed almost as a Latin typo. There is no 'light bearer,' and Lucifer is a Demon King whose powers bear no relevance to Christian fears.

In this era, we are damned by the grey morass of material that is found on the internet, ever clouding the truth. Meanwhile, the finest of academics are producing the best works of magickal research that have been written, eclipsing the texts from the late nineteenth and early twentieth centuries. No longer do occultists seek out ancient texts in places such as the British Library because the work has been done. The academics, while pointing out a distressing number of inconsistencies in the materials we all treasured, have now confirmed the discoveries we made through our practical explorations of magick. The demons we found to be true through experience, have been shown to be true through the newly discovered source materials.

For those of us who have worked with private grimoires, and those who have belonged to secret Orders and Temples, there is a clear divide between what is widely known and what is workable truth. A small number of modern occult authors have produced notable works, but many have repeated the errors that soil the internet. There is evidence of this in many places.

Have you seen the sigil of Lucifer? If not, or if magick is all new to you, come for a journey through these paragraphs and see how assumptions and presumptions have made people fall into self-delusion. For simplicity, let us say that a sigil is a drawn image, a seal, a signature if you like, that represents the spirit being summoned, and is said to support that summoning. I ask again whether you have seen the sigil of Lucifer, and you may believe you have, but I suspect that you are mistaken. What you have seen most probably looks something like this:

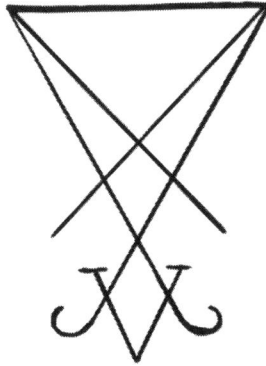

It may unsettle you to know this is a modern adaptation of a sigil that was, in more ancient times, drawn thus:

The more authentic drawing is disappointing, rushed, and not nearly so grand. It is little wonder that those seeking a powerful image to put in books first cleaned up the lines and made it more presentable. The modern version was further sanitized by subsequent authors, but may not reflect the original intent or content of the sigil.

In the *Grimorium Verum,* or *Grimoire Verum* (a sourcebook relied on heavily by those who seek the dark arts,) the artwork and sigils often appeared to be more like newspaper cartoons or childish drawings, than seals of magick, and the Lucifer sigil itself was a hapless scribble, as shown above. (In later editions, the 'tidy' sigil appeared, but earlier volumes showed the hurried-looking version.)

It might take your breath away to find that not only is the modern sigil a contrivance, but it is the sigil for Lucifer in Asia. The Sigil for Lucifer in Europe was drawn like this:

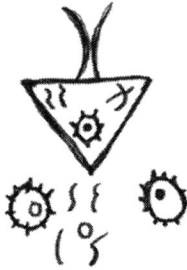

It was then cleaned up to look like this:

Admittedly, this isn't as pretty and doesn't look nearly so grand or dramatic, which may be why the Lucifer in Asia symbol is found on so many websites and pendants. It is claimed to be the one true sigil, even though it is the wrong one for anybody outside of Asia.

It has been argued that Lucifer in Asia may refer to the East in General, with Lucifer in Europe being The West. Where does that leave the Americas? From what point of view and from what location are East and West defined? Some would say Greece, where the underlying sources of the grimoire may have been written, but whatever the case, thankfully for us the grimoire goes even further with the required clarification, suggesting that Lucifer isn't called in the Americas at all. You are counseled to call Astaroth in America. Africa, meanwhile, is given over to Beelzebuth. For Americans, there is no Lucifer.

This is not what we believe, but it illustrates flaws in the sources that many occultists gaze upon with such reverence. People look to the *Grimoire Verum*, a relatively late grimoire in occult history, replete with errors and careless revisions, then handpick ideas while ignoring the tangible instructions of the texts. Books and websites continue to show the modern, clean Lucifer sigil, even though it bears little resemblance to the original, and works only for those residing in Asia.

If you study the *Grimoire Verum* you find that the Lucifer sigil is only one of the minor Lucifer 'characters,' and not the main image used in the grimoire. The Lucifer Pentacle in the grimoire is a series of lines within a circle.

This circle is the true symbol of Lucifer, according to the grimoire trusted by so many occultists. How is it, given all the evidence in the grimoire itself, that the image for Lucifer in Asia remains popular? Those clean lines look more like a logo or a brand, and I believe that is the only reason it is popular. It is easier to sell. It is, however, a modern bastardisation that can mislead the unwary and invite weak magick.

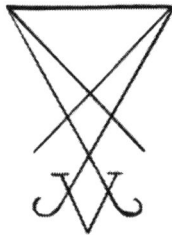

This sharp and elegant Lucifer in Asia sigil looks good on an altar but might be corrupting your magick and hampering your efforts to contact the true power of Lucifer.

It is flummoxing that with so many people turning to the *Grimoire Verum* for guidance, they miss the obvious statements made within the text itself. When taken at face value, the book tells us that all people living in The United States of America, attempting to contact Lucifer using the modern Lucifer in Asia sigil, are contacting a mere shadow of Lucifer, a shade or echo of the demon. What feels remarkable at first could be an illusion of power that will soon fade.

If you wish, do your own research to clarify what I have said here, but go to the primary sources, not the internet. A reading list is found at the end of this book.

As you may have gathered, I would never claim the *Grimoire Verum* to be an accurate, reliable or workable source, as it is based on many earlier grimoires, and found in sundry variations, collating more inaccuracies than most scholars can even follow. I have referenced it here to illustrate how easily people can be led astray by texts that appear to be accurate, even when they were revised and published in haste to satisfy readers during a period of history when there was a thirst for magick. The ancient texts were corrupted by profit seekers.

What are you meant to do when faced with such a confusing array of false symbols? Call to Lucifer and ask for your own sigil? That is an option and one that I have partaken of, finding it to be of little import. It is useful to look further back into occult history. You can find what you are looking for by consulting grimoires in private collections, and then seeking modern academic research. Perhaps the most ancient renderings of the sigils come from some five hundred years earlier, where they were drawn in *The Veritable Key of Solomon*. Read Skinner's book on the subject and you can see how the originals were gradually perverted into what is found in modern occultism.

This would all be nothing more than theoretical tittle-tattle, except that this reliance on sigils leads one away from the purity of Lucifer magick.

The Order discovered long ago that Lucifer can be called upon from any place in the world, regardless of your birth origins, without any sigil, and indeed it could be said that sigils connect you to egregores for Lucifer, rather than Lucifer himself.

In brief, an egregore is a pattern of consciousness, or a thoughtform, created through repetition, belief and sometimes a dusting of the supernatural. If a fraud describes a spirit or entity, and a sufficient number of people attempt to contact and work with that spirit for long enough, with sufficient commitment, for a particular purpose, in time that spirit takes on a level of reality. These manufactured spirits have their uses, much like servitors, but they can also be imposters.

When people use false magick to contact great spirits, such as Lucifer, what they get is at best a splinter of the original, a fragment channeled through an egregore. It may feel like Lucifer, and it may give you a strong sense of its reality. Egregores, once formed, want nothing more than your belief, because that is what sustains them, and so they offer sensations of supernatural contact. This does not mean they have the power to grant the wishes requested of them.

I find that people who connect with these egregores of the great demons become overly fascinated by them, too deeply attached, and before long they are worshipping them with love, feeding the egregore and obtaining little in return. The sigil shown at the beginning of this book connects you only to an egregore of Lucifer.

All that you have read may be confusing, disturbing, disruptive or if you are completely new to occultism, enough to make you think that magick and demon summoning is too much of an intellectual battlefield. It is not, and that will become clear.

I have not set out to confuse and dismay, but to illustrate to you that many occult certainties are nothing but delusions. Many of the techniques passed to the unwary are designed to give them false magick, where the demon gains more than the one seeking gain. There is much deception.

One of the accidents of modern occultism has been to disguise the true art, hiding it behind online forums and discussion groups, where gossip, chit-chat, and bombastic pretense occlude reality, guiding the unwary to misleading sources that include the wrong sigils, the weakest concepts, and the most debasing and ignorant ideas. We could say these are dark times for magick, but there is hope. For those who seek true magick and effective methods, everything you need is before you if you find a way to see what is already there.

Who am I to say these websites and forum loudmouths are wrong? Why should The Order of Unveiled Faces be taken any more seriously than those who slur, blur and conceal the truth? I will make no claim for the words given here but will illustrate through example and let you be the judge. You must judge me on the lucidity and efficacy of this magick, not on promises or projections.

If you research the subject at hand, understand that the book we use for obtaining contact with demons (which will be described shortly) must be read as an allegory. It is a code to be deciphered and understood in terms of symbolism. If contemplated without this in mind it reads as religious fanaticism rather than the pathway to demonic power. When you know it is a gateway, its secrets will come forth.

You are free to use the workings in this book without doing any further research or reading, and I believe that the sensations you will experience, and the presence of Lucifer, will convince you of the reality of magick. What I say about research only applies if you wish to understand how Orders such as ours arrive at our conclusions. If you want magick, the magick is here, and all you have to do is perform it as instructed.

The methods we have arrived at are not ours alone. Their reliability and accuracy have been confirmed through practice, results, and through the word of Lucifer. These claims of mine, however, should not be trusted but seen as our point of view. Their veracity can only be confirmed by your experience.

I do not speak for Lucifer, but I speak as one who stands at his side when working this magick. I do not speak for the demons revealed in this book, most of whom are hidden from the wider community of working occultists. I do not claim that myself, nor The Order of Unveiled Faces, are the primary authority on these workings. I urge you to be wary of anybody who makes such claims. Those who claim to be the one true source of knowledge always have a hidden agenda, which includes controlling you.

Any person who claims to speak for the demons, or have the demons speak through them, is somebody you should fear because that person has a weakness; a weakness that demands admiration and adoration. They are not a conduit for Lucifer or other demons, but a human ego in frantic need of approval.

Any human that seeks such worship is standing *between* you and Lucifer, blocking you from the demons and seeking to drain your strength through the demands of loyalty. Such people will offer warmth and love that makes you feel special while stripping away your ability to work magick for yourself. I suggest that you look beyond such people. Look beyond my

Order and me, and look into the magick itself with a wary and cautious mind, careful not to be taken in by frauds or false promises.

It is never wise to trust those who claim great lineage but show only a shallow and recent knowledge. Which is why, once more, I urge you to be skeptical of all, including myself and The Order of Unveiled Faces, and all who claim wisdom.

Skepticism is not the enemy of magick. If you are skeptical of our claims, you are wise. It is important to test the magick you receive. If you blindly follow the word of those who proclaim to know truths that you do not yet know, you are like the victim of a cult, led into self-imprisonment through the promise of illumination. Trust a bright and shining personality, and you are offering your energy to the vanity of a feeble ego. Such people, though weak, will leech you dry, until you are utterly reliant upon them. In magick, you should rely on nobody.

Read this book with an open but cautiously skeptical mind, prepared to work the magick as written should you choose to do so. Do not trust that we are the final authority or assume that we are masters appointed by some ridiculous non-existent brotherhood. You will know as you read what is true.

What we present here is offered to you. We cannot compel you to trust what is said here, but we can give you the option to research the subject yourself or take a leap of faith, or perhaps exploration, and move into the practice of magick, which is where the greatest truths are laid bare.

Do not abandon skepticism but put it aside for a while when performing the magick detailed in this book.

There are over a hundred demons here, but at the head of all the ranks is the shining light of Lucifer. When you sense the reality of Lucifer, you may feel a shiver, or sense the cold, white light, or something that feels like love, power, even destiny. You may sense strength and potential. I urge you to do this as your progress through the book, without overt expectation or demand. I urge you to do this now. Say the name of Lucifer out loud. You should be alone, and be daring enough to summon.

Contemplate the name of Lucifer, caring not what or who Lucifer may be (for now, for this brief time), and let yourself sense the shiver of his presence. Say his name. If you feel nothing, know that this is only your first step on a long road. The feelings will come to those who are able to work magick even if they do not come at once. There is nothing else you need to do for now. No offerings, no thanks, no protection. You have spoken his name and noted your reaction, which may have been strong or non-existent. That is enough.

It is true that many reading this book will already have a connection to Lucifer, or what they believe to be Lucifer. Others may never have cast even a rudimentary spell. The challenge of this text is to present our offering of magick in a way that makes it accessible to all readers. There is, we have found, no way to do such a thing. Magick cannot be made accessible to all. Magick is for those elected to work with its power.

Magick cannot be given to everybody because many minds are closed. (Skepticism is not a closed mind, but a curious mind. Remain curious and avoid being jaded.) Many people cannot move beyond fear or suspicion of evil and deception. Some will assume that demons are here to trick us with gifts and lead us to the Devil. Others will reject anything that doesn't agree with their previously sculptured opinions, rejecting what is said here out of hand without further thought or experience. About this, nothing can be done and nor should it be done.

We do not, therefore, set out to change opinions, to convince or to make this work accessible to all. The magick is accessible to those who are already open to the power of Lucifer and his demons. You will have some sense (I would dare to postulate) of what your place is in this larger picture. You should not accept anything I say on faith, but if you sense that there may be power in my words, read what is said, practice the magick as it is described and do not falter, quiver or tremble when the changes you seek come to pass.

Is any of this background material of importance, or would it be better to put all the bravado and declarations aside, heading into practical magick on page one? I will not delay any longer but do not feel that any student of magick, no matter how old, experienced or wet behind the ears, should proceed into the operations of magick without some forethought. All that has been said urges you to seek wisdom before results, and thus obtain results more readily.

The Requirement

I would like to acknowledge that my esteemed publisher, Christopher Wood, asked me to consider relaxing the tone of the opening chapter, and indeed the entire book. I am delighted that he made a request rather than putting his opinion forward as an editorial demand, and more so because he made this request before we had signed a contract. He is a bold negotiator and one that I respect. I politely declined to change a word. Christopher's response to my stance was one of laughter and glee. He said that readers would see that behind my words there is a gentleman with a genuine wish to share knowledge developed and cultivated over centuries (even though our Order only took up the challenge in the middle of the last century.) Such a delightful response, and one that I will treasure, though I would never claim to be a gentleman. I hope the magick will be more important than my personality.

I was convinced to write a paragraph on the first page, promoting the potential and detail of the major powers in this book. I am told that without such information, no reader would continue to read.

Christopher also questioned my use of the word 'hidden' in the title, because it suggests the demons have been deliberately concealed by some great and secret temple. I insist on the use of that word because the demons are hidden from ordinary people and most people who work with magick. For dabbling occultists, when you say 'demon,' they think of the seventy-two demons of the *Ars Goetia*. Others work with demons from grimoires such as *Grimoire Verum*, as described earlier.

Results can be obtained with such demons under certain circumstances, but with *Goetia* especially, the level of interference and clouding from egregores is high. (If you want to know the true names and origins of the seventy-two demons of *Goetia* you need to study extensively, and you will find that the popular internet listings are mostly based on Crowley's wildly inaccurate ramblings. More reading will be suggested at the end of the book for those with an interest in obtaining the true names.)

Many of the demons described here appear in demon dictionaries and encyclopedias, and many do not. In the source text that we use, there are errors, with some names being mixed, blended, cut off and corrupted. Their origins include languages as diverse as Hebrew, Arabic, Coptic, Chaldean, and Greek. Much of our work has involved direct contact with the four Demon Kings, who revealed the names and powers of the true demons to us, over time and with caution. These names and powers will be shared with you.

What we determined and came to know as true, was confirmed by academic research in recent years which almost entirely agrees with our work. The primary sources, previously lost (or hidden) brought light and confirmation to all that we have discovered. The details of this work will be covered in brief.

These demons are hidden from the public, and the method of working with them is largely unknown. Like many modern authors, I am pleased to say that our workings, although based on certain offshoots of ceremonial magick, do not require the ceremony. You will not be called upon to parade in an ermine cloak, waving a flaming wand of hazel. What you will be called upon to do is bring all of your focus into the magick of summoning.

There is some ease to be found with this magick and its practice. There are no Hebrew words to learn and no grand ceremonies. You will not be required to cast a circle, banish, cleanse or confess. You do not bind the spirits in an agony of submission but call them to perform the duties they are willing and destined to execute. When your desire is clear, the demons thrive on your desire and their existence is glorified by giving you what you ask for.

All that I have said is true, but I will not mince words. This book is not for the wholly uneducated, the ignorant, or fools unable to focus, concentrate and keep their mind on a subject long enough to understand what is being revealed. Put only the barest effort into learning this process, and you will not succeed. Commit to working as hard as is required and the magick will respond.

If the thought of such effort makes you shudder, settle down with your phone and distract yourself with something less valuable. The level of commitment and concentration required of you is utterly trivial compared to the effort you put into ordinary activities, daily struggles, petty arguments, and debates: I believe people put more effort into online disputes than they put into their magickal practice. If you want to succeed, that has to change. Find the space to know your mind.

Statistically speaking, it is likely that you have been poisoned by the device-based culture that addicts you into flipping through online posts, images, and other shallow distractions. I can assure you that if you continue with the addiction, you will remain distant from magick.

The Order of Unveiled Faces is far from a somber collective of old men who spend their time analyzing books. We live in the modern world, indulging in the pleasures, but we will not be enchanted into being slaves to some of the more destructive temptations. Our purpose is to enjoy life, to satisfy the self in deep and nourishing ways, and that means resisting some of the offerings in this world. Many of them are dehumanizing, and remove you from the very experience of life that is essential for magickal empowerment.

Concentration, imagination and the faculties of inner sight are all stifled by the onslaught of external stimuli. If your ears are plugged with music, your eyes filled with photographs and films, and your mind riddled with a thousand meaningless facts and opinions, you will not progress.

Do I describe an ascetic life where you are banned from Facebook, iPhones and other such delights, forced to wear a hair shirt and rise at dawn? I can assure you that I live in luxury, and I use Facebook every day to keep in touch with overseas family. I enjoy an occasional dollop of trivia. I will not, however, let it become a substitute for silence, patience, and the moment.

I am told that some people live their life as though preparing social media posts. When you become so deeply addicted to social media, you do not have an experience but experience the moment as though it will be your next post. When something is happening, you plan your post. You contemplate how to word it, rather than having the experience. This act of recording is the opposite of experience, and experience is your doorway into magick.

If you are old enough to look back to a time before such devices existed, examine how much of your inner life has been lost to distraction. Before these devices existed, did you daydream and wonder, and read, think, ponder and experience the world more? Would you rather see another photograph of somebody's lunch or spend some time preparing lunch for yourself, present in the moment of creation? If you are too young to remember a time before the era of the device, I challenge you to break your addiction for a few days and see what happens when you conquer the initial symptoms of withdrawal. You must be wise enough to know that this requires some time. Withdrawal can last days or weeks, but when you find yourself at peace with the place you stand in the world, looking out at your surroundings, rather than looking down at a screen, your imagination stands some chance of recovering.

I have heard many whimpers from those who say they are unable to visualize. This is nothing but a lie to the self. Every child knows how to daydream, and although the skill may be lost, daydreaming is an ability that you can recover if you give your brain a moment's rest from the persistent stimulation of images, noise, and ideas.

Read this passage of basic prose. 'In the afternoon he climbed the mountain and upon reaching its summit saw the moon sinking below the ocean to the West.' Do you have any idea what just happened? If you think our hero spent the afternoon driving through a city, you have a problem. If you know that our hero climbed the mountain and if you know what he saw, that is visualization. You seek nothing more than an understanding of the words. There is no glory in picturing visions more clearly than somebody else.

You may see the mountain, the hero's face, sensing the temperature, the scents, and other sensory delights that were not in the text. You may see nothing, only knowing what happened and what was seen and understood. You know he saw the moon. If you can read, you can visualize, and there is no requirement for further development of your imagination or concern that you don't have the ability to imagine. Whatever ability you have will, however, be stifled if you fill your brain with images and ideas that are more distraction than depth, which is why I warn against the addiction of thumbing through easy external imagery.

Images in your mind are more likely to be visual when they contain archetypes or meaning, and the imagery of our magick will do the work for you because it works with such archetypes. If you are instructed to imagine and can see nothing, then reading the words will be sufficient effort on your part to engage with the magick.

The Pathway

The rituals in this book use imagination, not to invent demons or create them as apparitions, but as a way of seeing beyond the ordinary. Imagination is the tool of the magician as much as it is that of an architect. There are some architects who craft a career without much imagination and manage to make more than a living wage, by relying on the culture of the average. I challenge you to engage with your imagination, no matter how ragged it may be, and put aside all claims that your imagination is not clear and bright enough for magick. If you are prone to be overly imaginative, I challenge you to reign in your fantasies and see only what is produced by ritual. I know that if you allow yourself to trust the method described forthwith you will discover that your imagination is a more potent tool than any grail, potion or philosopher's stone.

It is believed by followers of the works of Carl Jung and others, that humans have, whether literally or figuratively, a collective unconscious. Jung himself was surprised to discover this shared mind was patterned with images that were spiritual and universal in nature. During his experiments with Active Imagination, he discovered archetypes that appeared to be universal. Given the immensely broad range of interpretation of symbols, especially when related to an individual's personal life and experience, it seems a fiction to suggest that any symbols cross cultures, but this is what has been found. Jung has almost been dismissed as a mystic now, rather than a scientist, but his influence on our understanding of symbolism is important. Although each culture will have images that are entirely its own, there are archetypal images that appear to be embedded within humans.

For occultists, this is something that was discovered independently from Jung's psychoanalytical work, but you may find that if you read Jung's wilder works, such as *The Red Book*, his words do not read like a Freudian manual of therapy, but like esoteric texts. This is no coincidence because Jung was,

I believe, touching on the power of certain images that have effects on us that go beyond what is obviously contained in the image. A single image can trigger a sequence of events to come into being that otherwise would not have occurred. It is almost as though an image is a spell or a ritual in itself. When pictured in particular conditions, an image becomes a ritual.

By collating a series of images and working through them in order, almost like telling a story, you enact a powerful series of transferences through reality. It could even be said that all magick is an attempt to achieve this. Even a modest spell which appeals to a goddess is often more like a poem, replete with images that reflect the beliefs regarding said goddess. A call to angels in a ceremonial ritual may be occupied with obscure god names, but often contains archetypal images that sanction the working.

I should say here that when I say the word 'archetype' I am taking it further than Jung's concept of a peek into the collective unconscious. As occultists, we believe that there are images that transcend all human boundaries, powerful enough to be, in and of themselves, magickal. These images are your method for entering magick, and with a series of images in your mind, you can enact the most powerful magick. Imagery furnishes you with the ability to open a doorway to working with the great demons.

It may seem too simplistic to suggest that imagined situations can create magick, but it is the combination of chosen imagery that generates the effect.

To illustrate, let me take some of the imagery used in occult rituals and perform a light dissection. Wheat, the golden crop of life, is frequently described in rituals, and you are told to see yourself walking through fields of shining wheat. As with most images, there is more to this than the obvious depiction of moving through a source of life and light.

Wheat is utterly feeble. Depicted in many religious writings as a golden source of sustenance, in reality, wheat is a crop that is prone to disease. Its pathetic body crumples from a mere change in the weather. When lightning strikes, an entire field will burn. Wheat is easily trampled underfoot. When it does survive, wheat is crushed by the merest effort and turned into edible dust. A weed that was exploited for gain and consumption, wheat is a trivial nothingness. When you know the underlying imagery that is important to occultists, the image of walking through wheat becomes something different altogether. You do not walk through a wheat field in a trance of bliss while you feel at one with nature, but you march as one who has power over this feeble crop.

All such associations with imagery are completely subconscious, but they are stirred by the arrangement and presentation of the images. If told to imagine wheat, you may be deceived by its surface appearance of shining, wholesome goodness. If you are told to walk through wheat and trample it, then the imagery has a different effect. Your purpose is not to decipher the symbols in a described working (although if you have many years and sufficient curiosity you may do so), but it is to experience the images, in sequence, and let them work magick through you. The working is essentially effortless because it works with your connection to the collective unconscious. What your conscious mind may never know, your unconscious already knows, and this gives power to the images of magick.

If you have read much about occultism, you may know that a series of powerful images connected in this way can sometimes be referred to as Pathworking. When the New Age movement became a noticeable part of popular culture, during the 1970s and more blatantly and commercially during the 1980s, a handful of books emerged on the subject of Pathworking. The technique consisted of imagining a story in which you took part, travelling through strange and fanciful lands. You might, for example, be instructed to take yourself on a mental pilgrimage to obtain visions or personal change.

For occultists who had witnessed the dramas associated with the revelations of secret Pathworking methods utilised by infamous magickal Orders (or even for those who had merely heard of these dramas), decades before, such New Age bunkum was an insult to the great magick it weakly emulated.

In earlier times, Pathworking was a method employed by certain occultists to walk the paths on The Tree of Life mentally. It was considered an act of utmost secrecy and potential danger. If you have no concept of The Tree of Life or what it means to walk the thirty-two Paths, consider yourself fortunate to have saved some valuable time. Regardless of this, at the time, Pathworking was considered to be one of the great and secret keys. When people say that Pathworking was talked about in 'hushed whispers,' that is unquestionably true.

In many forms of this magick that subsequently arose from ceremonial Orders, a leader would orate a Pathworking much like a story, while the subjects would listen and imagine. Such group work was kept secret for many years.

As with so many matters, however, time gives great perspective. When the secrets of Pathworking were made public, the public didn't give a damn, and many fringe occultists were disappointed by workings that, now they were revealed, appeared to be trivial and outdated. A few experimental occultists did take note of the more potent aspects of the method and adapted the techniques to write their New Age books.

As the years passed it was revealed by academic research and open discussion, that Pathworking was not created by those infamous secret Orders. It came from much earlier times, and the method used to walk the paths on The Tree of Life was a modern corruption of an ancient technique. Many versions of the Pathworking technique were recounted by anthropologists throughout myriad ages and cultures. Once again, the assumption that a small group of upper-class Londoners held the great secrets of magick was revealed to be a falsehood.

Pathworking is not a technique that belongs to one order, and we must admit that it is a great irony that what was shown in some of those New Age books, although largely ineffectual, may have been closer to the techniques found worldwide in the magickal cultures of a rich assortment of societies.

There is not sufficient time, space or motivation for me to explore this further, except to say that applying the imagination to the act of taking a mental pilgrimage has been a part of magick for as long as magick has existed. I make this statement knowing that our great friend, the internet, will have many other ideas, and again, I would say that if you wish to do your research do it through the works of respected authors, not website babblers.

My experience of Pathworking was initially disappointing. I was fortunate to take part in a group ritual, led by a reasonably renowned occultist, and the underwhelm I gained from the experience (over several months) almost made me dismiss the technique as overstated in importance. Such perspective was invaluable because it meant I did not put value on the leader-student relationship. Pathworking, I discovered, is something that works best when worked by a solitary practitioner.

It was with some embarrassment that I used the methods from those denigrated New Age books to explore the magickal technique further. This left my mind open so that when I dedicated many years of my life to decoding the secrets of grimoires, I was able to recognise those rare places where Pathworking was being alluded to.

I cannot claim that the technique for demonic contact revealed by this book is mine or even that of The Order of Unveiled Faces, but I will say that we contributed to its rediscovery and the enhancement of a technique that echoes and rumbles throughout modern magick. Its structure is revealed in the source documents (discussed later,) and our purpose was to discern a way of working that method to aid communication with demons.

Pathworking is a form of mental journeying that is the fastest and most effective way to contact the great Demon Kings and their subordinates. It is not an exercise in fantasy, but the purest magick, and by telling a visual story to yourself, you connect with demons in a way that is a real as any elaborate evocation.

I have urged you to be skeptical, and I am certain that if you have any experience of magick, you will feel that my suggestion is a weak one. It would make more sense to have words of power, circles of magick, anointed candles, initiations, and admittance. I will say that this is like the difference between reading a book and performing a play. You can understand a story by reading a book. Seeing it performed on stage might produce a deeper sense of drama for you, but it is not required. You only need the story.

Pathworking is not a way of deceiving yourself but uses archetypes and magickal images that are so potent, your mind will be unable to resist them, and in taking these paths, only in your mind, a magickal connection will be made to your chosen demon.

When described plainly, this means that you imagine or read a description of a series of images, in which you are led to a place where the demon dwells. The journey is coloured with images that are the keys and doorways into magick. It sounds too simple to be real or effective and it is true that some perseverance with the technique may be required before you yield fully and let down the barriers that make it effective, but it is the most powerful way to make demonic contact, without danger of being possessed, obsessed, influenced or coerced.

The demons are called in a way that is pleasant to them, with a structure that makes them compelled to work with you because they have been approached in the correct manner. Far from wishing to harm, the demons wish to express their reality and can do so only when called by human desire. When approached with the secret images that give you access to their powers, the demons will never rebel.

The Pathworkings in this book were obtained by decoding the grimoires and their hidden imagery, confirming our findings through direct communication with the demons. There is no better way to source magick than through direct contact. Such work, when it becomes possible, surpasses all known texts. Further experimentation has shown that these

Pathworkings are a genuine method for obtaining contact that can be used by anybody.

The human imagination is powerful enough to motivate people to build cities and go on quests, but I can assure you that your imagination, even if suppressed somewhat, is almost infinitely crafty and able to work wonders. To prove this all you need to do is read a short piece of fiction and then analyze what went on in your brain. You are free to try this experiment, but to save you the effort I will show you what goes on in the mind of a person reading fiction.

When you read fiction, you do not receive a linear series of images that make immediate sense. Instead, you receive piecemeal information that is continually reevaluated and updated to create a coherent impression of the scene. This is an astonishing power of the brain to gradually create and destroy, leaving behind false images and keeping only those that apply. Read the following passage.

'He opened the door, and the room inside had a rosy glow, as though lit by a red lamp. He saw a skylight in the ceiling, stained red. There was no lamp, only the light from the filthy skylight. The walls were concrete, but traces of flowery wallpaper remained, as though somebody had scraped this underground room clean in a rush. The floor had no carpet, only soil. In the far corner, an armchair, and tied up there what appeared to be a woman, though it was difficult to tell in this light. Blonde hair poked out from a black velvet bag over her head.'

You now have a clear picture of the scene, but only because your brain built that scene as you read, discarding what was unnecessary. When you are first told the room appears to be lit by a red lamp, you may have actually imagined a red lamp. When you are told there is no lamp, but a red skylight, you discount the previous image. This process continues, with details being added and taken away. You were not informed that the room was underground, but once you know that, your impression of the room changes. You do not know there is an armchair with a woman in it until the end of the paragraph, but by that point, you have reassembled the scene in your mind. You come to picture the hero walking into this red-bathed room, seeing a blonde woman with a bag on her head, tied up in an armchair. If you had stopped reading halfway through, there would be no chair, no woman, just a reddish room. If you stopped reading just before the end, you would have no idea her hair was blonde.

Fiction writers present important images on top of each other, as rapidly as possible. If you read a scene such as the one above, and then the paragraph ends with, 'The pale man, who had been there all along, stood motionless, knife in hand,' you would feel confused or cheated. It wouldn't make sense. Writers of fiction craft their works so that the brain can just about keep up, without new information feeling incongruous. They allow the brain to reimagine the scene as we discover more, and this happens without our awareness of the changes, deletions, and crafting of the scene. All we see is the story and the completed scene. When recalling that scene, we never remember the mistakes we made at first. We remember the complete and coherent image that was formed by the end of the description.

This ability of the brain to form a coherent picture from images that are not all presented at once is remarkable, and very far from what is experienced when looking at a painting, or watching a film. This is why you will hear everybody from psychologists and occultists to artists and creative marketers, report that reading fiction is an essential exercise for the mind. Fiction is the material substance that fertilizes the mind and gives room for the growth of new ideas. Far from being a place where you entertain yourself with the images and ideas of another, it is a spawning ground for your imaginative abilities. The higher the quality of the fiction, the more refined the results, but even potboiler detective stories and romance novels exercise your imagination. Any fiction requires you to picture a series of events, with the manipulation described above happening in real-time, as you read. This develops your ability to use imagination in a creative and magickal way. If you want to develop your abilities as an occultist, read fiction.

Knowing this, however, we embarked upon a series of experiments aimed at exposing the flaws or challenges of Pathworking. To keep this story short, I will say that we discovered one of the most fundamentally difficult things to imagine is a straightforward journey without landmarks. That is, if you are told to imagine walking through a cave or tunnel, this is far more demanding than being told to imagine walking past a table, then a cat on a chair, and then an eagle in a cage. You can see how this works. When there are landmarks of symbology, it is easy to picture. When you are given a vague notion of what happens, as with walking through a cave, there is nothing to drive the imagination and nowhere to anchor or develop the images.

Unfortunately, most Pathworking is based on this idea of journeying from one place to another, often passing through long corridors or tunnels and opening doorways to see what is on the other side. Doorways are a problem for the imagination. In many rituals, you are told to imagine a doorway and then see whatever you see on the other side. Most people see nothing, and why should they? If you were reading fiction, you would be told what was on the other side, and you would imagine it as described. In occultism, it is a requirement at times, that images be allowed to arise by themselves, from nothingness, and that applies with our work also, but doorways, walking through fields and other images of movement, bring resistance. These journeys and blank canvases are extremely difficult to imagine and work with.

The solution we found was to present images that suggest the transformation of one place or state to another, without laboring over the journey itself. To illustrate, imagine a Pathworking that requires you to see yourself standing on a rocky plain, but then as you walk toward the mountains you see a tree in the distance, and when you get to the tree you see its branches are dripping with molten gold. This is a difficult thing to imagine because in reading this description, you know the ending before you get there. When you are standing on the rocky plain, in your mind, you already have the image of the dripping tree of metal in your mind, and so you are already there. As you mentally journey toward the tree in your imagination, your brain does the same thing it does when you are reading fiction; it fills in the blanks, jumping backward and forward through time to create a coherent scene. What you get then is not a journey or a sequence, but an impression of a scene. This is not effective enough to create a magickal event.

When reading fiction, the process is effortless and helpful, but when Pathworking it can make the process feel wrong if you suddenly find you are already at the tree, and then you are still journeying toward it, and then you try to see yourself approaching, but you already have a clear image of the tree and having arrived. Most people find Pathworking stressful not because they lack imagination, but because their brain creates a scene rather than a journey.

We found it was much easier to make statements of imagery in series, as follows:

You stand in a rock-strewn desert.
There are mountains on the horizon.
You stand at the base of the mountains.
There, a black tree, its bark scorched.
Silver oozes from the tree's green buds.
Liquid metal runs down twigs and branches, hardening around the roots like glittering ice.

In this example, no journey is described. There is no necessity to imagine moving from one place to another. The Pathworkings in this book are mostly less detailed than the one above. If you can picture those images, or merely understand what they mean as you read them, the magick will work.

Road movies, where two characters spend most of the film driving and talking, are popular because they don't show the characters moving. The characters stay in the same place on screen, in their seats, while the landscape around them changes. This is easy to watch. It is much more difficult to watch somebody walking from one place to another, and indeed, filmmakers frequently avoid this, showing only the first steps, and then cutting or cross-fading to the next location. Journeys are implied by cutting from one image to the next. This is the process we have chosen to use in magick.

A journey does not need to be experienced every step of the way, and a more effective Pathworking occurs if the connections are shortened, and you fade from one location or image to another.

In practice, this means you only need to read the images, without troubling yourself about the details of their content and meaning, or their connections. Pathworking has thus been simplified to the point where it can be carried out with extreme ease, even by those who claim to have no imagination and even by those with no ability to visualize.

You will notice that the imagery from Pathworkings overlap at times, with several demons sharing the same or similar imagery. No Pathworking is identical to any other, however, and if only one detail is different, that is sufficient to take you to the correct demon.

The wise amongst you will wonder about the pitfalls of repetition. If you have worked this imagery once, then you already know the endpoint. You know that you end up at the tree, so aren't you left with exactly the same problem, with the brain creating an overall scene with all the images at once? We have found that this is not the case. By presenting each image you can focus on that image, and although you will have a vague notion of where you are going in the Pathworking, you will have sufficient concentration and focus to remain with the image currently being called into your mind. You are not required to linger in these imaginary states, and therefore repetition does not weaken or interrupt this system.

This still leaves us with the problem of doors and empty spaces. Even in our method, there comes a time when you are told to leave space for the demon to join you. We have found the most effective way to do this is to focus more on the somatic feelings than the visual. In classic evocation, extreme effort is put into causing a demon to appear before you, whether in the room you stand, in a black mirror, or in a crystal or other darkly reflective surface. These visual evocations are so strenuous because they are filled with fear, resistance and are confrontational in nature.

Watch two business leaders meet (or World Leaders for that matter), and they will stand face-to-face, shaking hands, until the moment relaxes and they move to stand side by side, looking across at each other. The initial meeting is not confrontational, because it is eased by protocol, but if they remained standing face to face for long, it would become confrontational. The moment of relaxation is vital. In evocation, you call a demon to appear before you, without the ease of protocol, and no way to move aside or be freed, and this is indeed confrontational. It can convey resistance from yourself and arouse it within the demon. Standing before somebody is intimidating, either to yourself or the other, and direct eye contact is confrontational. It is reminiscent of two drunken thugs, facing off before the first punch is thrown. It can also lead to the opposite problem, where you are so confronted, you feel the need to bow, submit or yield to the demon.

Direct visual evocation has value but is not required. Many who strain to see demons are actually terrified of the demon's potential appearance and resist it, either consciously or subconsciously. Many 'successful' evocations are clouded and diminished by fear.

From the demon's point of view, to colloquialize the subject somewhat, it is similar to asking somebody you have just met to strip naked. You are calling a demon, who hides behind many layers of disguise and subterfuge, to be revealed in full. It is not something they are always willing to do upon first being asked to do so. Although 'holy' names can compel demons to appear in this way, even forcing them to modify their appearance to be 'comelier,' it is far better to avoid this confrontational dichotomy. Instead of trying to drag the demon before you, like a servant or slave, you can stand by its side, where there is a feeling of shared trust and power. What I have said here is allegorical, but should illustrate why direct visual evocation of a demon is often so difficult, and the alternative brings ease.

It is much easier to imagine a demon by your side. It is perhaps, even easier to imagine a demon behind you, but this I do not recommend as it can lead to fear and emotions that do not belong in the process. In our Pathworkings, then, you will be led to moments where you are in the place where the demon resides, and it is then easy to know that the demon is at your side. By taking the pressure off the visual requirement of the working, you are far more likely to sense the demon's presence than if you are trying to conjure up an image in front of you.

Magick is filled with irony, and it is another delightful irony that in relinquishing the need to see a demon, you are more likely to see a demon. Although you work only with your imagination, you are not creating imaginary fantasies, but recreating realities where demons reside. You may see, sense or know them.

The extent to which you are able to see or sense the demon has little bearing on the work you do with that demon. Pathworking is a way of summoning the demon, and then you must work with its strengths and attributes to bring about the result you desire. The demon will comply because it has a strong desire to fulfil its potential and manifest its powers in the world. What begins in your imagination can unlock magick that tears at the fabric of existence. In less dramatic words, this means you will get what you want if you are wise enough to know what you want and to choose the demons that can bring the change. What follows will give you more details on the nature of these workings, guiding you through this process, so that you summon with purpose and lucidity, to obtain the results you seek.

The Demonic Source

Our techniques, as revealed in this book, do not come from any source as recent as the *Grimoire Verum*, which was referenced earlier, but from a book much older. I reflected on the *Grimoire Verum* only to illustrate how the most corrupted sources are seen as truth and are misused by the poorly educated.

It may come as a surprise that the demons we work with are sourced from a book called *The Book of Abramelin*. It is known as *Abramelin* or *the Abramelin* for short.

When texts older than *Abramelin* exist – texts that reference Lucifer's existence directly, such as those mentioned earlier – why not use those to develop our magick? Unfortunately, they are all incomplete and do not contain magickal methods or true lists of demons. Although those texts did indeed contribute to our overall knowledge and research into Lucifer, *Abramelin* was the guiding light. We read everything, considered all, and used what mattered.

You may have heard that *the Abramelin* is most widely used as an instruction manual for contacting your Holy Guardian Angel. It is regarded as a religious text. Although it lists demons, it is not usually considered to be a demonic grimoire. This is a perfect case of a great secret being hidden in plain sight.

I can only urge you to read the book (using the latest translation by George Dehn and Steven Guth) to see how subtly and wonderfully its true intent is concealed and then revealed. A basic reading, made without looking below the surface, suggests that you must spend eighteen months in devout prayer to God before you can call your Guardian Angel forth and then bind the demons to do your bidding. The truth is that the religious instructions are an allegory for magickal techniques. God is not present in this work, but Lucifer is, and all the Hidden Demons are revealed.

Influenced in part by earlier works such as *Livre des Esperitz* and *Pseudomonarchia Daemonum*, this is not the earliest source, but it is not as corrupt and distorted as later texts such as *Grimoire Verum* that appeared hundreds of years later. Its most vital content comes from hidden sources, not fully traced, but reaching back to the most ancient magickal knowledge.

The book was chosen because we were led to it. We approached it from the perspective of those who sought to work with Lucifer and other demons, and were intrigued from the outset by the inclusion of the extensive demon listings, and the magickal workings in a book regarded as a 'holy' work.

The Abramelin was written sometime around 1400, listing hundreds of demons who are led by Lucifer, without the use of any sigils or seals. It is apparent that sigils were most likely invented by human hands later in time, in an attempt to divert attention to a method far from one that works most effectively.

The Book of Abramelin has been a guiding light in Western Occultism, but for reasons other than our own, and with its meaning overlooked by most readers. Aleister Crowley was so taken by the concept of the Holy Guardian Angel that he simplified the working of *the Abramelin* into his own Egyptian-laden version called *Liber Samekh*, which pushed together some of his favoured images with an old exorcism and other occult detritus, to create a ritual that became the cornerstone of his personal religion. Crowley, undoubtedly the most famous occultist of his time and ours, changed his mind about what the Guardian Angel was several times, sometimes believing it to be the higher self, and at other times sensing an entity beyond himself. Although these ideas were cluttered, vague and contradictory, they have been the keystone of occult practice for hundreds of thousands of working occultists.

It is possible that we are each granted an angel at birth that watches over us, but for every hundred souls claiming to have achieved the mythical Knowledge and Conversation of the Holy Guardian Angel as it so amusingly named, there are eighty that have lied, nineteen that have deceived themselves, and one that has gone mad. The angel may be there, but this operation, in which you spend eighteen months craving for

God, is better used as an allegorical description of magickal technique.

Lucifer and the Hidden Demons is our decoding of the indispensable magickal techniques and the most powerful and accessible demons that can be sourced from the book, while taking account of the mistakes made during its creation and translation, to create a complete system of magick.

Our initial work was time-consuming because the only English text in existence for most of our lives was the S. L. MacGregor Mathers translation, which was taken from a reasonable translation of a French text. The 1750 French volume he used was translated from the original German, but omitted and distorted the original work so severely one wonders how drunk or pathetic the translator must have been. Nevertheless, a bold attempt at the translation to English by Mathers in 1893, based on the substandard and incomplete translation, was all we had to work with. Despite its shortcomings, it retained power and allegory. The underlying message of magick was contained within its pages.

Our work developed, but with gaping holes. Through many years of experience with the demons, we sought more knowledge than was made clear in the text, developing a compendium of demons and the Pathworkings required for their calling. Our work strayed from the Mathers *Abramelin*, but the further it strayed the more effective our methods became.

Everything changed two decades ago when George Dehn compiled a German version of *the Abramelin* from the original sources, called *Buch Abramelin*. After many years of working with a mere reverberation of the work we knew to be true, we now had access to the information we needed. Even *Buch Abramelin* was found to be strewn with errors, and the later English translation (which appeared in 2006 from a collaboration with Steven Guth) also suffered from this problem, but the difference in quality and content was supreme when compared to Mathers. Every question, doubt or intrigue that was left regarding this work, was now opened to us. The most recent update to the book appeared in a 2015 edition, and if you choose to use it for further study, that is the one you should obtain.

The Order of Unveiled Faces set about working with what had been revealed to us directly by the demons, alongside what was revealed within the newly updated *Abramelin*, and we finalised a complete system of demon magick that we believe has no parallel. Do not trust this boast, but test it, give it scrutiny and judge the system on its actual effects and benefits.

The Magickal State

A difficulty faced by one attempting magick is the creation of a magickal atmosphere. Without this sense of magick being real and present in the moment, it is difficult to believe anything is happening. It is a stretch to convince oneself that magick is proceeding in an ordinary room in your home, by doing nothing more than closing your eyes and going on a journey within. When you set up an altar, with plentiful sigils, the light and smoke of candles and incense, it feels more like a piece of magickal theatre. It is easier to suspend disbelief in this state. This is, I am convinced, the reason for the structure of most Western magick. The dressings, cloaks, oils, gestures, words, mirrors, triangles, and daggers are presented and experienced as an act of preparation. It is a way of feeling and believing that the imminent magickal experiment is more serious, somber and real than a mere act of thinking or imagination.

The value placed on the correct mix of herbs, powders, magickal words, and sigils has led to an obsession with techniques that create patterns of questionable value beyond their theatrical content. There are occultists who would not consider performing a ritual without first taking a ceremonial bath (something that has always amused me), or anointing themselves with oil. These distractions are not even a blind to conceal something deeper, but dressings that support the work of the unimaginative, while concealing the nature of magick. Even the oil described in *the Abramelin* is of no use, beyond putting you in the mood for believing in magick. If you doubt me, know that some of its greatest proponents were pouring that oil over their heads in rituals, while using the wrong recipe for their entire lives. They hadn't read the modern and accurate translation provided by Dehn. The oil, so valued by Crowley and others, was fake.

You will be challenged by this book because there is no such rigmarole. It is easy to believe that if the magick all takes place in your head, then it is unreal, but I would reverse this and say that because it is in your head, it is the only reality. You can dress up an altar and make offerings until dawn, but unless you change on the inside, within your mind, in the quagmire of your emotions and perceptions, then nothing changes at all.

You are challenged to take on this magick in its purest form. If you feel you must light a candle, burn incense of sit before an altar, you can do so, but the less you do, the more focus you bring to the magick itself. I have seen hundreds of online photographs that people unwisely share, revealing the details of their altars, and even the finest look like an embarrassing corner of a thrift store, or the bedroom of an over-enthusiastic teenage witch.

For this magick, forget about altars. They belong in churches and cults. Instead, you sit in the corner of the room if you can, facing outward. No particular direction is of importance. I sit in an armchair, with the lights dimmed. You can sit against a wall if that is comfortable. You may also find that you prefer to stand, but I do not recommend lying down as it leads to overt daydreaming rather than Pathworking. Kneeling is too submissive.

The Pathworkings are most easily carried out with eyes closed, and yet the act of memorizing an entire Pathworking (which reads something like a short poem) is beyond the abilities of most. Although memory is a skill that has its place in magick, reading the words is more effective than learning and keeps a freshness within each Pathworking. I have seen people make audio recordings of the Pathworkings, or have others speak the workings for them, but none of this is necessary and is an encumbrance to the work. The technique is as easy as reading one sentence and closing your eyes, picturing what you have just read, and then reading the next sentence. When you read the final sentence and picture that image, you are in the place where the demon resides, and you can allow yourself to sense its presence.

You may choose to read aloud, or you can read silently. For some, the act of reading alone will generate the images, and there will be no need to pause and picture what has been stated. For others, it will be a requirement to pause and picture what has been read. The method does not demand perfection, and if you are forced to repeat a sentence until you can picture it clearly, you should consider this an acceptable part of the process.

For each demon you will find a description of their name, how it is most likely to be pronounced, with their specific powers and abilities. A Pathworking will follow these descriptions, and it is this Pathworking that you will use. The Pathworkings will appear as a simple list of descriptions. Simple as they may appear, such images will reveal themselves to be more than the fragments of broken poetry that they appear to be. A full explanation of all that is required to summon the demons will be delivered in due course, but you now have some understanding of our methods. Nothing you do, say, chant, enact, burn or consume can have as much influence on the malleable fringes of supernatural reality than the use of imagination, and in Pathworking you will find (or gradually discover,) a source of magickal practice that transcends all others.

Naming Conventions

The earlier discussion on sources established that the names in our book are not always the most ancient, although in most cases they are. Each name was finalised and certified as effective through exhaustive research and experience. Working to move beyond Mathers' mistakes, we were able to contact the demons with sufficient clarity to ascertain their true names and have our suppositions confirmed by using those names.

When the 2001 translation of *Abramelin* was published, it confirmed our work, but also led us to make some adjustments. What you find here is our version of the names based on experience with the work of *the Abramelin* in its most complete form, considering all our experience alongside new knowledge and subsequent experience.

It should be remembered that the author of the book, Abraham of Worms, was a German Jew, with extensive knowledge of Hebrew, Greek, and other languages. His background and native language will have influenced the way he reported the names. We believe that he did not write the names letter-by-letter, but used his knowledge of the sound of the names to write vocalisations that worked in German. A degree of explanation and elaboration is required when it comes to pronunciation, given this personal interpretation of the names.

You may think it is a superior practice to read the words as you see them, and if so you are entitled to experiment with such an approach, but the pronunciations are elaborated upon here for precision and to account for our knowledge of the sounds Abraham of Worms implied in his writings.

When you see the name Lucifer, you know how to say that name without reading a phonetic approximation such as LOO-SIFF-URR. A name such as Leviathan may cause more confusion. Is LEV pronounced as in LEVER or LEFT? This is why we will include a pronunciation outline for each name.

The third Demon is often listed as Satan, usually pronounced as SAY-TAN or SAY-TUN. Through experience and based on the origins of the name, we believe Abraham of Worms was using the name Shahtan, which has a different pronunciation altogether. Shahtan is a Demon King and not the Devil of The Bible, any more than Lucifer is. We believe that using the older version of the name, based largely on Hebrew texts, helps break that association with the Devil. When you call on Shahtan, you are not burdened by childhood fears of some imaginary horned beast.

The fourth King is Belial, and without guidance, you might assume this name is pronounced BEE-LIE-AL. With a knowledge of the original texts and a combination of German and Hebrew sources (and our involvement with the demon), it becomes palpably clear that BELL-EE-AL is more accurate.

Let us not forget, however, that working with imperfect names for many years, we achieved great wonders, and thus meticulous pronunciation is not mandatory. The Pathworking associated with the demon is of far greater importance. I need say no more on the subject and trust you will recall this when using the magick.

The Abramelin lists hundreds of demons, but some are not easy to work with, and others appear to be composite names, corruptions or errors. We do not list every demon from *The Abramelin*, because they are not all of practical use. We list over a hundred Demon Kings, Dukes and their Servants, with their powers, correct pronunciations and the Pathworking required to summon each.

The demons listed differ from Mathers greatly, and to the Dehn edition only when our experience with a demon has guided us to know the true name. If you prefer to work with the names as found in Dehn, the instructions provided for each demon will work, and you will find the names only differ by one letter or sound, and only in rare cases.

Some of the names will be familiar to you if you've worked with the occult before, and it can be a trial to relinquish preconceptions. Asmodi, to provide a single example, is widely known as Asmodeus and you may be startled that the name is different here. When the name appears as Asmodeus in so many texts, including *The Book of Tobit* and *The Testament of Solomon*, and even at some points in the Dehn translation of *The Abramelin*, why would we use Asmodi? In every case, the convention of naming has been guided by experience, feedback and the quality of results obtained. If you have never read about magick before, this will be of no concern, but if you know a thousand demon names, it may take some effort to use the names here with comfort.

The most provident way to work with these materials is to let go of prior knowledge or experience and attempt to reach the demons using the procedures given. Even should you have already summoned Lucifer, or any demon, with success, I urge you to see how dissimilar and expansive the experience is when using the procedures delivered by The Order of Unveiled Faces.

Do not let yourself be burdened by familiar names, conventions, and traditions, but allow yourself to enter the magick as though you are a beginner. A sense of wonder and expectation will lead you directly into the magick, where fear, doubts, and logical cogitations will hinder your progress.

Perspective on The Demons

There are various ranks of demons in this system but do not think you should always seek out the most high-ranking demon for every solution. If magick could be performed with such a brutish lack of subtlety, this book would list Lucifer alone. The matter of ranking is, for the most part, organizational. The exception is that the Demons Kings and the Dukes of Lucifer have powers that are more far-reaching and life-changing. This may not be what you need in many situations. You will become aware, as you read about the demons and their powers, that some are wholly inappropriate for minor needs, and a demon which presents as less powerful may give you the accuracy you require. You do not break a butterfly on a wheel.

The Four Demon Kings

The highest order encompasses the Four Demon Kings, being Lucifer, Leviathan, Shahtan, and Belial. Lucifer is called in all workings.

The Eight Dukes of Lucifer

The Eight Dukes of Lucifer are Astaroth, Asmodi, Oriens, Ariton, Magoth, Beelzebub, Paymon, and Amaymon.

The demons that follow may be classed lesser demons, and they come in three ranks. The first rank of lesser demons work under the combined governance of Oriens, Paymon, Ariton, and Amaymon. Each of these lesser demons is summoned by first calling on Lucifer, who will grant you permission to perform the Pathworkings for the governing Dukes, namely Oriens, Paymon, Ariton, and Amaymon, before finally working the path to the demon that serves them. These demons are listed here:

The Demon Servants of
Oriens, Paymon, Ariton, and Amaymon

Moreh, Frasis, Myrmo, Trapis, Parelit, Obedemah, Hasperim, Fasma, Nogah, Ethanim, Melabed, Apolion, Asturel, Hagrion, Liriol, Asorega, Ragaras, Ilekal, Sarasim, Sigis, Laralos, Ipakol, Balabos, Nolom, and Amillis

The next rank works under the governance of two Dukes. To summon these demons, you first summon Lucifer, who grants you permission to perform the Pathworking for the two governing Dukes, before finally calling the lesser demon. There are three such groupings, as follows:

The Demon Servants of
Astaroth and Asmodi

Lagiros, Ugalis, Dagulez, Bialod, Ranar, Buriub, Nimalon, Bagalon, Anamalon, and Sagarez.

The Demon Servants of
Asmodi and Magoth

Kela, Diopes, Magyros, Lamargos, and Disolel.

The Demon Servants of
Amaymon and Ariton

Harog, Agebol, Rigolen, Irasomin, and Elafon

The final ranking of lesser demons each work under a single Duke. To summon these demons, you first summon Lucifer, who grants you permission to perform the Pathworking for the governing Duke, before finally calling the lesser demon. The demons are as follows:

The Demon Servants of Astaroth

Iromenis, Apormanos, Ombalafa, Kataron, Iloson, Kalotes, and Golog.

The Demon Servants of Asmodi

Maggid, Gillamon, Ybarion, Bakaron, Presfees, Hyla, and Ormion.

The Demon Servants of Oriens

Gagarin, Sarsiel, Sorosoma, Zagal, and Turitil.

The Demon Servants of Ariton

Nilion, Maranaton, Calamosi, Rosaran, and Semeot.

The Demon Servants of Magoth

Tagora, Corocon, Dulid, Arakison, and Daglus.

The Demon Servants of Beelzebub

Diralisin, Camalon, Bilek, Corilon, Borob, and Gramon.

The Demon Servants of Paymon

Sumuron, Ebaron, Zalomes, Takaros, and Zugola.

The Demon Servants of Amaymon

Akorok, Dalep, Bariol, Cargosik, and Nilima.

Summoning these lesser demons requires more time and effort because in some cases you will be required to complete six Pathworkings. You should remember that you are not calling a minor spirit, but a legion of spirits that are working in harmony.

Moreh, for example, works with the power granted by the four Dukes, and Lucifer above. Takaros works with the power of Paymon and Lucifer. The lesser spirits can be far more defined and prevailing, and although the work required to obtain contact with them is lengthy when compared to a brief summoning of Lucifer, the wise choose to work with these 'lesser' demons more often then they work directly with Dukes and Kings.

You may also wish to know that when you summon Lucifer to command lesser demons, the other three Demon Kings (Leviathan, Shahtan, and Belial) are brought to bear on the problem, guiding the demons that they influence, but you are not required to call the other Kings as the coordination of power is conducted by Lucifer. You only summon the other three Demon Kings directly when you wish to access their particular powers.

When reading about the influences and offices of the demons in the following chapters, you will understand the appeal of each spirit, and why its strategic implementation may be what you need.

In reading what has gone before you should understand that there are numerous ways to select a demon to satisfy your desires. There is a key to choosing your demon and the appropriate power in the later chapters, but what follows is an elucidation of the summoning itself.

Summoning Demons

In this chapter, I will explain the workings of the ritual in precise but brief detail. The ritual is uncomplicated and will not be made ornate for the sake of appearance.

When summoning a demon, you will be told, for example, 'First summon Lucifer. Then summon Oriens. Then summon Paymon,' and so forth. This is evidently straightforward, but you will subsequently find in the instructions for summoning Oriens, Paymon, et al., that you are instructed to 'First summon Lucifer.' This does not mean you summon Lucifer twice. In any ritual, you only summon Lucifer once, when commencing the work. Summon Lucifer, and then summon each demon, without a repetition of the Lucifer summoning. If, for example, you are told to 'First summon Lucifer. Then summon Astaroth. Then summon Asmodi, before proceeding to summon Lagiros,' that would mean you summon Lucifer, and then when you come to the page describing Astaroth you ignore the instruction to summon Lucifer because you have already done so. In the plainest terms, you summon Lucifer once only at the beginning of each ritual.

This may cause you to wonder why it is stated that you should, 'First summon Lucifer,' for each demon, if this is something you then omit. The instruction to summon Lucifer is given for those occasions when, for example, you are working with a single demon. You may choose to work with Astaroth. Should you seek to work with that Duke, the instructions read, 'First summon Lucifer. Proceed to summon Astaroth.' In such a case you would first summon Lucifer and then summon Astaroth. The instruction is provided for consistency, clarity, and as a reminder that each ritual begins with a Lucifer summoning. It does not mean that you call Lucifer at each stage of a combined ritual. If you are summoning six demons, you call Lucifer only once, and then summon the remainder, in order, without repetition of the Lucifer call.

The ritual should be performed in private, in a place where you are able to bring calm focus to your working. Silence is not required, but you should not work in a place where other people are making noise, or with music or entertainment soiling the atmosphere. Sitting in an armchair in the evening is my choice, but you may prefer to work at first light, in the cold of an outdoor morning. The requirement is that you are able to bring your attention to the ritual and keep it there for the duration. Any time of day or night is acceptable, and other considerations such as astrological correspondences are irrelevant.

Know what you want, and why. The demons may question you, either through voice or by probing your feelings, intentions, and beliefs. You may or may not sense this, but they are seeking clarity within your desire.

Do not enter into the ritual with uncertainty, unless the purpose of your ritual is to resolve uncertainty. Know what you desire, be it a manifestation of results, expanded knowledge, greater self-awareness or a straightforward curse. Know what you want so unmistakably that when confronted by a demon you do not stumble or hesitate to make your request known clearly and honestly.

Although you should be clear in your request, place no restrictions on the manner of the manifestation of the result. Should you wish disease upon another, do not limit the potential of the magick by selecting a particular disease. Your desire should be clear, but not limited in scope. Ask for disease, and you will spread disease. Ask for a specific illness, and you reduce the creative impulse of the demons to find the fastest and most direct pathway to the result. Some balance is required. A vague desire is not as powerful as a precise one, but explicit precision becomes limitation. Impose only as much precision as is required to bring you satisfaction. No more and no less.

To begin the summoning, there is no preliminary invocation, call, gesture or other symbolic action because there is no doubt in your mind what is taking place. Ceremony is not required because you know you are summoning a demon, and you do not need any call to ancient gods, permission from angels or a declaration of intent. Close your eyes and know the demon or demons you are about to call. Consider their names and know they are aware of your intent from this moment. You do not require a physical description of the demon's appearance, nor a sigil. You only need the name and the Pathworking. The intention to make contact is more powerful than you may believe, and so the act of sitting down with the intent to perform magick is one of the most powerful aspects of this magick. Magick is about intentions made incarnate and so the intention to connect institutes the connection.

To reiterate, because it is of paramount significance, know that you intend to connect with the chosen demon (or demons.) This is your intention. You will summon a demon and make a request, and the demon will answer your call because you have chosen a demon who wishes to raise itself into reality by expressing its powers.

In the work that follows, know that you can use the English written here, or you can translate anything from this book into your native language. You may prefer, for example, to translate the Pathworkings into your language, if it is not English. When you speak to the demon, use your own language. Keep the demon names as they are written in this book, but use the language that is easiest for you to speak. Magick books are often filled with Latin rituals and chants because many of the grimoires used by occultists were translated into Latin from other languages. It is important to know that these translations occurred in relatively modern times (just a few hundred years ago), long after the early source materials were written. Latin is no more magickal than any other language. A handful of uneducated occultists claim that demons 'speak Latin' suggesting it is their language of choice, but this is incorrect and makes little sense given that the demons were named long before the appearance of Latin texts. Demons will understand you if you speak in your native tongue. They are less likely to understand you if you have no idea what you are saying, so don't waste your time translating anything into Latin.

You now perform the Pathworking, and this is as straightforward as described earlier. You read each line of text in the Pathworking, and allow the image to be as clear as it can be. If you see nothing, you see nothing. Your eyes may be open, closed, or open to read and then closed as you imagine. Let this be effortless. Straining to create an image only makes the image elude you. Read the sentence, within your mind rather than aloud. Each image takes you to a place and then on to the next place until you arrive at a location where the demon is already present.

To illustrate with the summoning of Lucifer, you would first read the sentence, 'You stand in a rock-strewn desert,' and you know this or imagine it, and this is where your journey begins.

You then read, 'There are mountains on the horizon,' and in seeing or knowing these mountains you do not yet journey to them, but allow them to remain on the horizon. The next sentence tells you that, 'You stand at the base of the mountains.' Without picturing the journey, the new image is created, and you see yourself at the base of the mountain. You may 'see' through your own eyes, or you may see yourself from a distance, from above, or from any combination of these, or you may see nothing and merely know that you are at the base of the mountains.

What, you may wonder, should these mountains look like? Are they surrounded by grassy foothills and meadows, rising to snow-capped peaks, or are they shattered cliffs and black rock that obscure everything but the starlight above them? The information given in each line is sufficient to create the journey. The images you choose, or that are chosen by your subconscious, or offered by the demon (for the demon may now be reaching to you just as you are reaching to the demon) will be correct. Any time wasted on debating on the quality or suitability of the images is time wasted.

You are now told, 'There, a black tree, its bark scorched.' The use of the word 'there' means that no further journey is implied. You are still at the base of these mountains. If you find that you move to another location at the base of the mountains, allow it. The remainder of the description is not a journey but a clarification of your destination. 'Silver oozes from the tree's green buds. Liquid metal runs down twigs and branches, hardening around the roots like glittering ice.' You may picture the liquid metal as silver as mercury, or red and steaming like liquid steel. The particulars of the image do not matter, but in establishing this image, you solidify the destination. Having done so, you are now in the presence of Lucifer.

As an aside, I will say that most Pathworkings are considerably simpler than this, and may only present two or three images. Be confident that in reading these sentences, despite their simplicity and lack of detail, you are being taken on the required journey to reach the demon's domain.

To complete the summoning, you only need to say the name of the demon, out loud or in your mind. Here you would say, 'Lucifer,' and you know that Lucifer is by your side.

What occurs now is rarely the same from summoning to summoning, but you will usually sense the demon's presence by your side. Demons will usually be on your left. There are rare exceptions, but in most summonings, the demon will appear on your left, sometimes slightly behind you. It does not matter that you are seated against a wall, because you are, in reality, in the location specified by the Pathworking far more than you are in any ordinary room.

If you are gifted with imagination, you may turn to see Lucifer who can appear as anything from a child bathed in moonlight, to a man of huge stature with translucent skin and a beautiful face, or something as abstract as a star. You may see something more monstrous. Whatever you see is Lucifer. There is no need to 'test' the demon. In many traditions, there are near-endless orations and tests to force the demon to convince you it is the correct demon. These trials are no way to start a relationship of power, and due to the Pathworking, they are not required. No other demon could reside here.

You may not sense Lucifer's presence, or what you sense may be extremely vague, to the extent that you wonder if you are convincing yourself erroneously. Ignore such doubts, and indeed do not feel a need for an experience of the demon. The extent to which you perceive the demon varies from person to person, and from summoning to summoning. You summon the demon, and the demon is present. Now you make your request.

No matter how dramatic or undramatic the experience, do not prostrate yourself before the demon in worship. Some do this out of a desire to obtain the demon's compliance, and others because they are awed by the experience. Your purpose in summoning the demon is not to worship (any more than you would worship a dentist, shopkeeper or another provider of service) but to communicate your request.

Speaking to a demon is straightforward, although it is understandable if you find it unusual in the beginning. You may feel that you are talking to nothing, with doubt and a feeling of foolishness coming before your desire, or you may be struck with awe and fear. Speaking to the demon can occur within your mind, or you may speak out loud. If the demon responds with a voice heard in the room, or in your mind, resist fear. You summoned the demon, and if it requests more from you in the way of clarity, or probes you for information, you should give this freely.

The demon will not ask for any pact, deal or offering, and if you feel that it has done so, know that you have deluded yourself. The desire to make offerings comes from a deep fear that we are subservient to demons. Resist this, and know that the demon would not make such demands when summoned through a Pathworking. In most summonings, you will make your request, and you will sense an acknowledgement from the demon. You don't sense a promise, but an acceptance of the request. At this point, you can bring the ritual to its conclusion (which will be described in due course.)

In most of these rituals, your request will be to obtain access to the lower spirits. If, for example, you are choosing to work with the King Belial, your request would be, 'Lucifer, I ask that you allow me to summon Belial,' and you would then perform the Pathworking for Belial, speaking your actual request to Belial. The phrase 'allow me' is rather colloquial, but effective. If you prefer to say, 'Lucifer, I ask that you grant me the power to summon Belial,' that is also effective. You can use your own wording if the intention is the same. For the remainder of this book, I will use the phrase 'allow me' as I believe it gives respect and flow to the working, without being too deferential to any demon.

In some rituals, this sequence can go on for some time, with authority being assigned through several demons. Were you to call Hasperim you would do so by asking Lucifer to allow you to summon Oriens, Paymon, Ariton, Amaymon, and Hasperim. You would then summon Oriens, and ask Oriens to allow you to summon Hasperim. You would then summon Paymon, and again, you would ask to be allowed to summon Hasperim. This would be repeated for Ariton and Amaymon, summing each demon with a Pathworking, and asking that you be allowed to summon Hasperim. You would then perform the Pathworking for Hasperim, making your actual request - the one that will solve your problem - to Hasperim. These longer rituals do require more time, but the request you make is extremely simple, and therefore less demanding than you may imagine.

You can speak in ordinary words, without the need for phrases such as, 'Oh mighty Lord, I humbly request that thou hear my call.' Speaking in a clear and precise manner that makes sense to you is better than aiming for some pseudoarchaic prattle. One unblemished sentence may be all that is required to communicate your desire. In the following chapter, I will illustrate a ritual with a walkthrough to clarify an example of how this may occur.

With your request made, you should wait to see if the demon asks more of you or gives acknowledgement. If a few moments pass and you feel nothing, continue. This may mean calling the next demon in a sequence, or if you are finished, it will mean closing the ritual as will be described.

The demon may or may not make itself known to you. Any demon's appearance, should it become visible at any point during the ritual, will be unique to you and may change over time. Do not be misled by demon dictionaries that insist a particular demon will have three heads or will always look a certain way. The demon may emanate power, love, anger, beauty and many other sensations, but the visual appearance, although it may at times be monstrous, is usually abstract (such as light), or even quite human. In all cases, what you see is not an illusion, but your current interpretation of the demon based on emotions, sensations, fears, hopes, preconceptions and the nature of your imagination. You may find that a demon takes on a more stable appearance after being summoned several times.

You should not at any time or with any demon make a bargain or promise to the demon, nor any offering, as all such trade is created by an illusion of the human mind plagued by fear, and not by any demon. If you believe a demon has made a request, remind yourself that this is your mind playing tricks, and ignore the request. If the demon becomes insistent, you can ask the demon if it is willing to help you with your request. It will answer in the affirmative. If it does not, this means your fear has got the better of you and is clouding your connection to the demon. You should close the ritual (as described shortly) and attempt this at another time.

The demons do not make demands. Do not be afraid of such occurrences because they are extremely rare and only delay your magick. Never fear that this will offend the demon because the demon will see that you were being led by fear, not clarity. The demons want the clarity of your desire so that it can be fulfilled.

There is a belief amongst demon worshippers that you must make offerings to the demons. No physical offering is required, and may indeed be repulsive to the demon. What the demon wants is to fulfil its destiny, and that is achieved by helping you obtain what you desire. When you get what you want, that is what the demon wants. It is a partnership of power. You do not control the demon and it does not control you.

No sacrifice, slaughter or offering is required, although there seems to be a desperation amongst occultists to offer up blood, alcohol, food and other scraps of unwanted matter. Only the fearful make such offerings, to appease the demons, but they do so in error.

An altar strewn with food and candles is a filthy place where alcohol evaporates and food goes stale. A sigil smeared with blood is not a delicious feast but a form of assault.

Many occultists believe the demons feast on such putrid offerings, but there is no truth in this. A glass of whiskey left out will merely evaporate. Bread will shrink because it has gone stale. If you see the alcohol moving strangely around the rim of your glass as though being sipped, it is because of surface tension and the evaporation of alcohol on glass. It happens to any ordinary glass of whiskey that goes left undrunk. Do not delude yourself into thinking physical offerings are of any interest to the demons. What appears to be consumption is an illusion that you perceive because you are too eager for proof.

The offering you must make is the honesty of yourself and your ambitions, and the choice to work in a symbiotic relationship, giving a demon the destiny it craves. Anything else you offer is like throwing cabbage leaves at the feet of a King.

When you feel that you have said enough, you close the ritual and return to your ordinary world. To do this, you give thanks and then use a reversed and shortened form of the Pathworking. You do not need to list all the demons you have called. You only thank Lucifer and the final demon. In the above example, you would say, 'Hasperim, I thank you. Lucifer, I thank you.' You can use a different phrase of similar tone, but this is elaborate enough. If you have called only to Lucifer, then you thank only Lucifer. In all cases, your final words of thanks should be to Lucifer. If you have called many demons, as in the Hasperim example, do not think that you are ignoring the other demons. You have called a legion together, and in giving thanks to the lowest demon, and then to Lucifer, your feelings of gratitude are communicated to all.

Speak without levity or gravity, and give no heed to the results you seek. You thank the demons only for being present and for hearing your request. Thanking a demon for a result before it has happened is presumption and in a ritual context can feel aggressive and demanding. Thank the demon with a simple phrase, for hearing you, and allow yourself to leave the demon in peace. You do not give it license to depart, as you are the one departing from its presence, and you certainly don't banish, as the demon should not be pushed out of your life.

To reverse the Pathworking, you only need to read the first image of Lucifer's Pathworking, aloud or in your head, and this will return you to the place from where you began. That image will always be, 'You stand in a rock-strewn desert.' Allow this image to be as clear as it can be, and if you see nothing, merely know that you stand in a rock-strewn desert.

To close the ritual completely, you become aware of the ordinary world, your eyes open, your awareness extending to the reality around you. Most of the time, your location will suddenly appear to be extremely mundane and ordinary, and this can be an unpleasant jolt back into reality. This should be allowed, but then rise from your chair, or move from where you are standing, and continue with your day. If you find that reality does not feel ordinary, that is also acceptable, but you should set the magick aside. Put the book away, move from the location where the magick was performed, and partake of a commonplace activity. This act of moving on from the magick is how the ritual is closed, and although it lacks theatrical impact, it is more effective than any gestures, rites, power words or ceremony.

A summoning may take only a few seconds, although in some cases you may build a rapport where you speak with the demon for some time, or where you wish to remain in its presence for longer. Do not become too fascinated with the demons. To do so is like giving into infatuation before understanding the underlying feelings you have for somebody. Fascination and adoration weaken you. Respect the demons, but do not worship. To worship is to make yourself seem so small to the demon that fulfilling your wishes is of little import. When you remain strong and true to yourself, you appear as somebody who will appreciate and revel in results, and the demon will be eager to bring what it is that you have asked for. The results you wish for will be brought about in whatever way they can be because this is the demon's desire as much as it is yours.

Although magick can and will fail when you ask for too many changes, or changes you resist on an internal level, if you ask wisely, as has been instructed throughout this book, you will get results.

For any given problem you need only summon the demon and make your request once. To summon repeatedly in an attempt to increase the power or magnify your connection to the demon is like asking a restaurant to hurry up with your meal; they will most likely spit on your steak. Harass the demons when they are already at work on your problem, and you will appear weak and less appealing to work with.

If the situation continues to be a problem, this does not mean the magick has failed. Everything is undergoing continual change, and even a successful ritual may be subject to the apparent return of a problem. In such a situation do not insult the demon by believing the ritual failed, but summon again and treat this as a new situation. You may even find that an apparent failure guides you to choose a different and more suitable demon, or to adapt your request as the situation changes. In most circumstances, none of this applies. You make your request and the demon complies; you get what you want. In most cases, summon once and let that be all.

An exception to this, and one that occurs especially when summoning Lucifer, is when you work with a demon on a developing situation that requires you to direct magick efforts as the situation develops. In most situations you curse, the person suffers, and that is all you need. In some situations, you may require many ongoing changes because the situation is large, complex and (most importantly) changing and adapting. In such situations, you may summon as often as daily, seeking the demon's advice or making new requests as the situation develops. Never summon for the sake of summoning, but only when you need guidance or to cause additional change. It may be daily, or it may be once a month or less. This is an advanced form of summoning and should be used when magick is definitely working. It should not be used when you are fearful that your rituals lack power, but when you are confident they are working. In most cases, you can keep it simple and summon once. The more complex and ongoing summoning is something that becomes possible when you are confident and familiar with summoning. For most readers, it may never be required. When you can summon once and get what you want, you would be a fool to waste more time on anything with greater complexity.

If a demon's power does not match your desire or the nature of the sought result exactly, recall that in theory, any demon can achieve whatever is asked, so a close match will be sufficient for your needs.

For more complex problems you may find it is effective to call two or more demons to work on a single problem or to achieve a desired result. It may be that several individual powers are required to achieve a complex effect. In such cases, summon each demon on a separate, consecutive day, making your request to each demon. Let each demon know that you will also be summoning (or have already summoned) other demons, and name them, to ensure harmony in the working. You can tell each demon the overall result you seek, and then make a request for the part you want that demon to play in obtaining the result. This level of complexity is rarely required. In ninety-nine percent of cases, I believe you can call a single demon, using the power most likely to achieve the result, and trust that it will be enough. Only summon more than one demon if you have analyzed the problem and remain convinced that a combination of powers is appropriate. Never assume that combining demons in this way is inherently more powerful. It runs the risk of bringing confusion, which can reduce power. It is only more powerful when the powers will be able to bring harmony to your intention. This style of work should be carried out only when you are already familiar with summoning and have achieved some success with the demons.

If there are several issues that you wish to address with magick, do not be tempted to perform rituals for them all at once or you may attract too many changes, or lose the focus to act on your intentions. When a legion of demons is revealed, there can be a temptation to perform thirty rituals over thirty days, to clear up your life. Use restraint and allow several days to pass between each ritual. There is no set time limit, and nobody can stop you from performing eight rituals in a day, but seeking so many different results is like pulling on all a puppet's strings at once. The result will not be coordinated. Approach a problem, make your request to the demons, allow some time to pass and then approach a new problem or situation.

An Illustrated Working

To illustrate what may have until this point sounded abstract, I will show how one might call a demon for a specific purpose. This will include the summoning of Lucifer and a Demon Duke of Lucifer. By illustrating one example, you should be empowered to work with the information in this book to structure any ritual with ease.

In this ritual let us say that you are calling Calamosi, a Demon Servant of Ariton. Your purpose is to bring justice to those who have worked against you. We will assume that an unknown and unnamed enemy has caused problems for your business, and you wish to bring justice to that enemy. Justice comes in many forms, but when requested of a demon it will mean that one who works against you can no longer work against you.

In order to call Calamosi, you must first summon Lucifer, then Ariton, before summoning Calamosi to make your request.

When you are ready to begin your ritual, you perform the Pathworking for Lucifer as set out later in the book. You have seen this already, and it appears as follows:

You stand in a rock-strewn desert.
There are mountains on the horizon.
You stand at the base of the mountains.
There, a black tree, its bark scorched.
Silver oozes from the tree's green buds. Liquid metal runs down twigs and branches, hardening around the roots like glittering ice.

When you have imagined the final image, Lucifer is beside you. Say, or think, the name Lucifer. It is wise to allow a moment to sense Lucifer, but do not be disheartened if no presence is felt. If Lucifer speaks to you, answer, in your mind or with words, but remain clear about your purpose, which is to summon Ariton and thus Calamosi to achieve justice. You say, 'Lucifer, I ask that you allow me to summon Ariton and Calamosi,' or words to that effect.

You may sense that your request has been granted, or you may feel nothing. Often, you will sense Lucifer withdraw, and this is not a sign that you have been abandoned but that you have been heard. Whatever occurs, or even if nothing appears to occur, you now summon Ariton with this Pathworking:

A pond of milky water.
Pink blossom falls into bloody mud.
A decaying forest green with moss.

Now say, or think the name Ariton, and as before, you allow some time to sense Ariton, who is now by your side, but regardless of the experience you remain focussed on your purpose and say, 'Ariton, I ask that you allow me to summon Calamosi.' You do not need to justify or explain to any demon why you are making this request unless the demon asks. Should Ariton ask why you wish to speak to Calamosi, give your honest answer. You may sense nothing further, or you may feel a clear sensation of permission. In most rituals, there is little to no sensation, and it is relatively rare for a demon to question your motives if they are clear. Any such questioning is not a denial but gives you the opportunity to clarify and continue.

Allow yourself to feel confident that you now have permission to summon Calamosi and perform the Pathworking as follows:

The scorched remains of a forest at dawn.
Smoke leaking from a broken rock.
A breeze that smells of raw fish, salt and seaweed.
A lone tree in an endless meadow.

When you picture yourself by that lone tree in the endless meadow, or when you say or think the words, you are in the location where Calamosi resides. Say, or think, the name Calamosi to complete the summoning. Your request may then be as simple as, 'Bring justice to the enemies that have worked against my business.'

You may prefer to add more detail, explaining the harm that has come and how you have felt, but do this only to provide information, not justification. It is like giving a statement to the police. You provide evidence that they can work with but you do not perform the investigation or make the arrest.

The degree to which you elaborate will be a personal matter, but for most the wording can be brief. If you are seeking information, you may spend more time in the ritual, listening for an answer, impression or omen that gives you an answer. If nothing is revealed, know that it will be in due course.

You should not rush the ritual but do not be dismayed if you reach this point, make your request and sense the demon withdraw. You have been heard, and there is no need to continue with anything more ostentatious. If you sense nothing, know that your request is genuine and has been heard and that lingering in the ritual is not required. Be confident, and close the ritual. You always thank the final demon, and Lucifer, so you would say, 'Calamosi, I thank you. Lucifer, I thank you.' Even if the demons have withdrawn, this should always be said. You do not thank the intermediary demons (in this case, Ariton.)

You now reverse the Pathworking. You only need to read the first image from Lucifer's summoning, and this will return you to the place from which you began. That image will always be, 'You stand in a rock-strewn desert.'

You now become aware of the ordinary world, eyes open, and the ritual is complete. Should you hear additional noises or experience sensations that could be described as supernatural, do not fear or reject them, but welcome them as an initiation into the reality of magick. If nothing happens, be patient, and let the results prove the power of the magick you have performed.

Your Pathway to The Demons

It has been claimed that every demon has the power to do anything you ask of it, but each has a specialty, office or power that makes it the most appropriate choice for the issue you choose to address. It could also be said that most people can hold a paintbrush, but how many can paint a portrait, and how many could create a masterpiece? In selecting a demon, you are finding the spirit who can create a masterpiece from the challenge of your situation.

It is tempting to become ensnared in speculation about the nature and origin of demons, attempting to ascertain their meaning and purpose in your life. I am of the opinion that when you perform magick that summons a demon through Pathworking, you will gain a definite sense of the demons that surpasses the speculation of all theologians.

I would not deter you from research into this subject but should warn you that every document is as incomplete as this one when it comes to the philosophy of demons, and you may find that expressing and developing your purpose and pleasure is more important than answering mystical questions that may, inevitably, be unanswerable.

Having selected a problem or situation that requires magickal influence, you are required to choose a demon most appropriate to match the essence of the result.

The following short chapters are a key to finding the demon you wish to work with. You may choose to read the book and search for the power you need by gaining a complete understanding of each demon, but the following pages should make it easier to find the power you need.

I also recommend that you read through all the powers of The Demon Kings and Dukes before beginning any magickal work. These can be found in the chapters The Four Demon Kings and The Eight Dukes of Lucifer

The categories on the following pages are:

To Manipulate Reality

Influence, Compelling, and Controlling

Financial Situations

Sex, Passion, and Seduction

Persuasion, Charm, and Trust

Healing and The Body

Guidance and Wisdom

To Find Peace

Legal Problems and Justice

Willpower and Personality

Protection and Binding

Personal Skills and Creativity

Corruption and Cursing

Causing Disease and Injury

For Mental Suffering

To Create Illusion.

Having found the name of the demon you think will be appropriate you can use the contents page (or the Search function within an e-book) to find that demon, and check the full description of its powers, to be certain they match your desire.

To Manipulate Reality

To make a situation reach its conclusion more rapidly, by manipulating time – Lucifer

Cause chaos, confusion, and mistrust in a situation – Leviathan

Discover and intensify psychic and magickal abilities – Shahtan

Undermine all stability in somebody's life – Belial

Influence, Compelling, and Controlling

To make somebody succumb to temptation. - Asmodi

To compel somebody to decide swiftly and in your favour. - Parelit

Cause somebody to doubt their magickal abilities. - Nolom

Cause arguments and mistrust within a group. - Amillis

To tempt somebody into being disloyal. - Bialod

To influence through the calm power of your voice. - Buriub

Make a competitor waste money. - Nimalon

Compel somebody to feel remorse for their actions. - Ombalafa

Make a competitor face unexpected disruption during a key business opportunity - Ombalafa

To quieten noisy people, including neighbours. - Nilion

Create harmony in a workplace you manage - Nilion

To cause somebody to feel submissive in your presence - Maranaton

Make your partner more loving - Maranaton

Compel somebody to pay what they owe - Tagora

Cause a competitor to believe they have done all that can be done, to make them relax too much - Tagora

To compel a person to leave their home, workplace, or any other position - Camalon

To cause one person to be violent to another - Camalon

Cause somebody to change their mind or reverse a decision - Bilek

To make those who work for you respectful and obedient – Bilek

To make a lover faithful – Takaros

Force somebody to reveal secrets they planned to keep – Takaros

To win competitions by influencing judges – Zugola

To quell an argument and bring peace – Zugola

Financial Situations

To overcome feelings of poverty and resentment – Oriens

To make somebody forget what you owe them – Moreh

To find a stable job – Ethanim

To request a growth in your income – Melabed

Request money for a specific purpose – Diopes

To become a well of new ideas with financial potential – Magyros

For an increase in luck when gambling – Iromenis

Bring financial loss to those who build their success on your work, ideas or reputation – Iromenis

To find an emergency source of money – Maggid

To encourage people to bestow gifts upon you – Maggid

To obtain approval or agreement from financial superiors – Gagarin

To get the best deal when buying or selling – Gagarin

Sex, Passion, and Seduction

To attract another with direct will – Astaroth

To attract another through an appearance of calm power – Ugalis

To arouse sexual thoughts in others when you speak – Anamalon

To radiate sexual potency through your gaze – Sagarez

To make a lover more experimental and disinhibited – Lamargos

Discover the depths of your sexuality – Apormanos

To increase chance meetings that lead to sexual and emotional attraction. – Apormanos

To cause one you desire to feel passion for you – Daglus

To make a disinterested lover passionate – Daglus

Cause somebody to have sexual dreams about you – Kalotes

To take the energy and vitality of another during sex – Iloson

Persuasion, Charm, and Trust

Speak with clarity and confidence – Ranar

To make somebody feel in awe of you – Bagalon

To be seen as an authority – Golog

To improve your reputation amongst all who speak of you – Golog

To make somebody trust everything you say – Gillamon

To make a group of people believe you are worthy of attention and investment – Gillamon

To open communication – Diralisin

Cause communication to be clear and honest – Kataron

Healing and The Body

To bring relief from pain. – Corocon

To encourage fertility – Corocon

To heal injury and sickness in an animal – Dulid

To endure pain with bravery until healing occurs – Dulid

To break an addiction – Arakison

To limit the effects of disease and illness – Arakison

Guidance and Wisdom

Discover what you want from your life – Paymon

Detect the intentions of an enemy or competitor – Balabos

Discover somebody's true thoughts – Apolion

Find answers to difficult problems – Myrmo

Sense what the future holds – Ebaron

To find that which is lost – Ebaron

To uncover secrets that affect you – Zalomes

To outwit those who steal your ideas – Zalomes

Discover the most peaceful solution – Dalep

To break out of current patterns – Dalep

To Find Peace

Emerge from a crisis unharmed – Amaymon

Bring peace to a home or environment – Frasis

Recover emotionally from a setback – Irasomin

Overcome thoughts that torment you – Calamosi

Legal Problems and Justice

To make you calm and clear-minded when pressured by intense questioning – Asturel

To be seen as innocent by all who hear you speak – Trapis

To bring fortune in a legal situation – Rosaran

To let others see the deception in a fraud – Rosaran

To crush the ambitions of somebody who wishes to defeat you in a legal argument – Corilon

Bring justice to those who have worked against you – Calamosi

Willpower and Personality

Find balance between self-esteem and ego – Elafon

Improve your willpower – Bariol

Find balance between optimism and negativity – Nilima

To find courage – Nilima

Embrace the power of patience – Bariol

Protection and Binding

To protect your home and possessions – Obedemah

To break a known curse, even when somebody has made a link to you – Hagrion

To remove the will to curse – Ipakol

To bind a person, so they are unable to work against you – Liriol

Banish spirits that have been sent to torment you – Nogah

Protect those that you care about – Sigis

Discover the true name of somebody who works against you in secret – Asorega

To protect against accidents – Harog

To protect against attack when traveling – Agebol

Make somebody unable to perform magick clearly – Akorok

Make an enemy feel sympathy for you – Cargosik

To clear and charm a new home – Cargosik

To remove traces of yourself from a home – Akorok

Personal Skills and Creativity

Learn to perceive when people are speaking the truth – Ilekal

To improve artistry, craftworking, or creative expression – Kataron

Become skilled at listening – Iloson

Learn fast and easily – Kalotes

Overcome nerves and anxiety in high-pressure situations – Semeot

To improve lucid dreams and astral experiences – Borob

To discover gifts and abilities – Sumuron

Find inspiration for creative projects – Sumuron

To improve a skill in a short period of time – Corilon

Discover new ways of working – Semeot

Corruption and Cursing

Strike fear into anybody who considers challenging you – Ariton

To make two people feel disgusted with each other – Laralos

To make somebody lose their source of wealth – Ragaras

Make a competitor suffer from a poor reputation – Hasperim

Make an enemy's business fail – Bakaron

To make somebody suffer in the way they made you suffer – Presfees

To enable a never-ending cycle of misfortune – Sarsiel

To expose somebody's secrets or cause them to be apprehended for their crimes – Sorosoma

To cause those who deceive you to contract an illness – Sorosoma

To cause mistrust within any relationship – Bakaron

To cause a person to act recklessly – Presfees

Causing Disease and Injury

To cause somebody to suffer accidental injury – Sarasim

To cause minor ailments to occur continually – Disolel

To bring sickness of the bowels – Zagal

To cause insomnia and nightmares – Zagal

Bring disease that causes scars, blemishes and other forms of ugliness - Sarsiel

For Mental Suffering

Cause somebody to lose all hope – Magoth

Cause somebody to be paranoid – Fasma

To fill somebody with uncontrollable anger – Lagiros

To fill somebody with self-loathing – Kela

To cause a person to feel anxious about a situation – Rigolen

To make a person doubt a plan – Hyla

Make somebody forgetful – Hyla

Cause somebody to experience panic and anxiety – Turitil

To make somebody feel like a fraud – Turitil

To Create Illusion

To create an increase in personal beauty – Beelzebub

To appear younger – Dagulez

Make something ordinary appear special and desirable – Ybarion

Make somebody think they are more talented than they are – Ybarion

Cause people to remember what they like about you – Ormion

Become less visible – Ormion

To create an air of dignity – Gramon

Attract fame through magickal glamour – Gramon

Make an enemy believe they have already won – Diralisin

Create a veil over an object or place, so nobody looks there – Borob

The Four Demon Kings

The Demon Kings are led by Lucifer, and it is Lucifer that oversees all the operations and magickal procedures in this book. Lucifer is summoned at the beginning of every ritual, in order to grant access to the other demons. You can also summon Lucifer directly and work with his power, as described in the following pages. There is an additional chapter at the end of the book called *Working with Lucifer*, which presents more detail on the scope of Lucifer's direct powers.

The four Demon Kings are summoned for life-changing events, or times when you need colossal transformation and are willing to accept disruption and rescripting of your life.

To call the other Kings, you would say, 'Lucifer, I ask that you allow me to summon Belial,' or whichever Demon King you have chosen. You would then perform the Pathworking to summon Belial to make your request.

Lucifer

No demon can be called without first summoning Lucifer. Even the three Demon Kings that accompany him are under his command. This hierarchy is not one of oppression and subjugation, but trust and cooperation. When Lucifer chooses to work with you, it is because you have called him to do so, and the other demons willingly fall in at his side.

To make a situation reach its conclusion more rapidly, by manipulating time.

There will be more detail regarding Lucifer and his powers at the end of the book. The powers are too extensive for a brief summary. Here, the summoning of Lucifer is described so you can use the above-named power, and also so that you can summon other demons.

Lucifer is pronounced as LOOSE-IF-UR. LOOSE as in LOOSE. IF as in IF. UR as in BURN. If you have a preferred or more familiar pronunciation, use that, and it will work.

Summon Lucifer with this Pathworking.

The Pathworking of Lucifer

You stand in a rock-strewn desert.
There are mountains on the horizon.
You stand at the base of the mountains.
There, a black tree, its bark scorched.
Silver oozes from the tree's green buds. Liquid metal runs down twigs and branches, hardening around the roots like glittering ice.

Leviathan

Leviathan has been portrayed in legends as a sea monster, but this is allegorical, and the Demon King usually has a presence that is anything but monstrous.

To cause chaos, confusion, and mistrust.

The Demon King can be called to bring all three of these situations to bear on a person or situation. You can cause a leader to suffer mistrust, confusion and a series of chaotic happenings, from accidents to misunderstandings. If you require a lesser effect, you may ask for mistrust alone, or confusion, rather than all three powers. Leviathan works with a power that feels like rage, and the effects will be extreme. Be aware that if you are close to the person you have attacked, you may be affected by the aftershocks.

Leviathan is pronounced as LEV-EYE-ATH-AN. LEV as in LEVITATE. EYE as in EYE. ATH as in MATH. AN as in AN.

Summon Lucifer, and then proceed to summon Leviathan.

<u>The Pathworking of Leviathan</u>

You stand at the edge of a stagnant lake.
The bones of a bird on the floor of a rotting forest.
A flat, grassy land with ocean in the distance.
The ocean rages with a lightning storm overhead.

Shahtan

This name is often given as Satan, which is either an uncomfortable name, or can mean something else altogether if you are a Satanist. Here, we profess that Satan is one of the Four Demon Kings, and that when pronounced correctly, his name is Shahtan. This is confirmed in Chaldean, Hebrew, Coptic and Gnostic texts. You can say the name Satan if you prefer but the emotional, religious and psychological connotations of that name are problematic and conjure preconceived notions of evil. The Pathworking ensures that whatever name is used, you contact the correct spirit.

Discover and intensify psychic and magickal abilities.

Shahtan is most pleased to grant you greater magickal ability. This may require you to work harder, increasing your ability to concentrate and imagine, or Shahtan may imbue you with a sense of magickal prowess that brings order and strength to your rituals. If you are working to improve your psychic ability, Shahtan will intensify your efforts and clarify your results.

Shahtan is pronounced as SHA-TAN. SHA as in SHARP. TAN as in TANK.

Summon Lucifer, and then proceed to summon Shahtan.

The Pathworking of Shahtan

You stand in a field of flaming wheat.
Fresh blood on a shattered rock.
In a sandy field a circle of flames surrounds a fallen tree.
The tree collapses to silvery ash and red embers.

Belial

Belial is described in ways too numerous to explain, across many textual sources, but is often associated with powers of hostility, and the ability to stimulate guilt and bring weakness. The demon's presence is often difficult to detect, but the results are usually fast and disruptive.

Undermine stability in the mind and heart.

This power may sound similar to that of Leviathan, but it is not directed at chaos and confusion, but at disrupting feelings and thoughts. When your intention is to bring intensive disruption to the stability of a person, or group of people, Belial will remove stability. The victim of such attacks will be weakened in both the mind and heart so that feelings cannot be used to support the mind, and the mind cannot be used to overcome feelings. Nobody can meditate their way out of this level of attack.

Belial is pronounced as BELL-EE-AL. BELL as in BELL. EE as in SEE. AL as in BALANCE.

Summon Lucifer, and then proceed to summon Belial.

The Pathworking of Belial

You stand on a frosted field of grass under clouded moonlight.
At the edge of a stream there are splinters of gold.
Morning lightens the sky to an overcast grey.
By a towering black rockface snow falls onto stony ground.

The Eight Dukes of Lucifer

The eight Demon Dukes of Lucifer offer immense power without causing great disruption.

To summon a Duke of Lucifer, you must first summon Lucifer and ask Lucifer to grant you the power to summon the named demon. You may, for example, summon Lucifer and then say, 'Lucifer, I ask that you allow me to summon Astaroth.' Upon summoning Astaroth, you would then make your request directly to Astaroth as described in *Summoning the Demons*. This process is the same for all the Dukes of Lucifer.

Astaroth

To attract another with direct will.

When you wish to make somebody attracted to you, using willpower rather than charm or natural attraction, this is the ritual you would use. It can be used to make somebody feel attraction they would not otherwise feel and can be used in all manner of relationships, from business to personal.

Astaroth is pronounced as ASS-TAR-OATH or more easily as ASS-TAR-OTH. ASS as in MASS. TAR as in TARGET. OATH as in the word OATH, or OTH as in MOTH.

First summon Lucifer. Proceed to summon Astaroth.

The Pathworking of Astaroth

In a dark part of the forest, shards of amber in the soil.
The bones of a bat on a slab of granite.
The entrance to a black cave billows yellow, sulphurous smoke.

Asmodi

To make somebody succumb to temptation.
When you know somebody is tempted by a situation or desire, and they are trying to resist, Asmodi will compel that person to weaken and succumb to temptation. If there is no temptation for the demon to work with, it will have no effect.

To tempt others into doing things they don't want to do.
While the first power is more about making somebody give into their craving, addictions, and obsessions, this power is used to make somebody act in a way that goes against their personal and moral values, or against their better judgment. Somebody may, for example, decide not to sign a contract but this ritual could make them sign it, even though they will then be filled with regret. Or somebody may choose not to be with a certain person, or choose a particular job, but you can compel them to do what you want them to do.

Asmodi is pronounced as AZZ-MO-DEE. AZZ as in JAZZ. MO as in MOAN. DEE as in DEEP.

First summon Lucifer. Proceed to summon Asmodi.

<u>The Pathworking of Asmodi</u>

An iron chain hangs between two trees.
The sky flashes with silent lightening.
In a field of dead grass, three trees bloom with white blossom.

Oriens

To overcome feelings of poverty and resentment.

In order to become wealthy, or even to begin a journey to greater income, the feeling of poverty must be left behind. This does not mean you should convince yourself that you are rich already. The ritual can remove the feeling of being born poor and unworthy, making room for a more beneficial alternative emotion. Resentment of those with more wealth anchors you to poverty, so you can ask Oriens to release this resentment enabling you to see the power and prowess of those who have succeeded. This makes it easier to emulate them and draw in your own wealth.

Oriens is pronounced as OAR-EE-ENS. OAR as in BOAR. EE as in SEE. ENS as in TENS.

First summon Lucifer. Proceed to summon Oriens.

The Pathworking of Oriens

At sunrise a crow pecks at the body of a dog.
A white dove, dead but unstained, in the mud.
Within a flaming forest, you stand in a cool stream.

Ariton

Strike fear into anybody who considers challenging you.
There are many ways to curse, but this power is used when you
believe somebody is about to challenge you, in personal affairs,
in business or in any situation where there is an imbalance of
power. If somebody is about to challenge you, or opens a
challenge (for your job, your partner, or anything else) this
ritual will fill them with sickening fear, bringing the challenge
to an end.

Ariton is pronounced as ARE-REE-TORN. ARE as in ARE. REE
as in REED. TORN as in TORN. (You will notice this makes the
R sound twice and brings a different rhythm than may be
obvious when reading the name as written English. You may
simplify it if you wish.)

First summon Lucifer. Proceed to summon Ariton.

The Pathworking of Ariton

A pond of milky water.
Pink blossom falls into bloody mud.
A decaying forest green with moss.

Magoth

Cause somebody to lose all hope.
The power is as basic as it sounds, making the person you name lose hope. This does not guarantee they will become depressed or incapable; some people continue to function without hope. Removing hope does, however, make a person less ambitious, less of a challenge, and weaker in many ways that can be useful.

Magoth is pronounced as MAG-OTH. MAG as in MAGNET. OTH as in MOTH.

First summon Lucifer. Proceed to summon Magoth.

The Pathworking of Magoth

A circle of fire surrounds a standing stone.
An old naked man points at the ground.
A full moon over a still, black pond.

Beelzebub

To create an increase in personal beauty.
Although you can ask Beelzebub to make somebody else more beautiful, perhaps to make a current partner easier on the eye, the power is usually used to increase your own beauty. People will notice a change in you, often suspecting you are in good health or have lost weight. The initial glow will continue to intensify with the results of this ritual being expressed and expanded upon over several months.

Beelzebub is pronounced as BEE-ELL-ZEE-BUB. This pronunciation is familiar to most. BEE as in BEE. ELL as in TELL. ZEE as in SEE with Z replacing S. BUB as it sounds.

First summon Lucifer. Proceed to summon Beelzebub.

The Pathworking of Beelzebub

In the dawn sky a single bright star.
A young boy points at the star with a silver dagger.
The red sun rises over snowy mountains.
You stand at the base of the mountains, in shadow.
White flowers grow between the black cinders on the ground.

Paymon

Discover what you want from your life.

When you know what you want it is easier to obtain than when you are floundering from one desire to another. The ritual may give you insight into where you want to be in twenty years, or at the end of your life, but often it will give insight into the very next steps you should take. Then, a year later, you may perform this summoning once more, and a clearer, more long-term picture will arise. The answers you seek may come during the ritual, but if not they will occur to you over the weeks that follow.

Paymon is pronounced as PAY-MUN. PAY as in PAY. MUN as in MUNDANE. Some prefer to pronounce this as PAY-MOURN.

First summon Lucifer. Proceed to summon Paymon.

The Pathworking of Paymon

A white horse is motionless on the opposite bank of a rushing river.
A toad struggles over dry, cracked earth.
A wall of cracked rocks holds back the dark ocean.

Amaymon

Emerge from a crisis unharmed.
When a crisis is at hand, you may think it will be difficult to find the time to perform magick, but as you become familiar with the demons, you will find that in times of crisis their support brings great warmth and comfort. This power means that no matter how the crisis unfolds, and this may be personal, financial, on any scale, you will emerge from it as a whole and strong person, able to recover and reestablish your life.

Amaymon is pronounced as AM-AY-MOURN. AM as in JAM. AY as in PAY. MOURN as in MOURN. Some prefer AM-AY-MUN where MUN sounds like the first part of Monday (MUN-DAY.)

First summon Lucifer. Proceed to summon Amaymon.

The Pathworking of Amaymon

A huge standing stone in the forest is covered in ivy.
A full moon over a field of gravel and thistles.
At the edge of a stagnant lake there is a rusted sword.

The Demon Servants of Oriens, Paymon, Ariton, and Amaymon

To summon the Demon Servants of Oriens, Paymon, Ariton, and Amaymon, you must first summon Lucifer and ask Lucifer to grant you the power to summon the named Demon Dukes and Demon Servant.

If you were summoning Frasis, you would say, 'Lucifer, I ask that you allow me to summon Oriens, Paymon, Ariton, Amaymon, and Frasis.'

You would then summon Oriens and ask to be allowed to summon Frasis. You would say, 'Oriens, I ask that you allow me to summon Frasis.' You would then use the Pathworking to summon Paymon and say, 'Paymon, I ask that you allow me to summon Frasis.' You repeat this process with Ariton and Amaymon, before performing the Pathworking to summon Frasis.

With Frasis now summoned, you would make your request directly to Frasis. This process is the same for all the Demon Servants of Oriens, Paymon, Ariton, and Amaymon, listed in this section.

Moreh

Under Oriens, Paymon, Ariton, and Amaymon

To make somebody forget what you owe them.
If you owe somebody money, this ritual can make that person forget, or lose the will to seek the money from you. If you owe several people, name them all in the ritual. When you are going up against a large, automated system, such as the computer records in a bank, you should direct your request at the bank itself, as an entity. The effects are stronger when aimed at specific people, but you can get creative results even when challenging large organisations.

Moreh is pronounced as MORE-EH. MORE as in MORE. EH as the E sound in LET (without the L or T.)

First summon Lucifer. Then summon Oriens. Then summon Paymon. Then summon Ariton. Then summon Amaymon, before proceeding to summon Moreh.

The Pathworking of Moreh

From a grassy hillside you see fire in the green forest below.
The water of the lake is stained with blood.
A white tree grows at the edge of the lake, its roots stained by the bloody water.

Frasis

Under Oriens, Paymon, Ariton, and Amaymon

Bring peace to a home or environment.
Useful when moving into a new home or workplace, it is most effective if performed in that place. If you cannot gain access to perform a ritual, you can still ask for Frasis to make a place, such as your office, to become more peaceful. The power is most effective with new beginnings, but can also bring peace to an environment that has deteriorated, or appears to be stained with negative energy.

Frasis is pronounced as FRA-SIS. FRA as in FRAY. SIS as in SISTER.

First summon Lucifer. Then summon Oriens. Then summon Paymon. Then summon Ariton. Then summon Amaymon, before proceeding to summon Frasis.

The Pathworking of Frasis

An old forest where every tree has died and turned the colour of ash.
Milk is poured into the soil.
In a brilliant green field of grass there is a single tree, red and autumnal, leaves pulled away by the breeze.

Myrmo

Under Oriens, Paymon, Ariton, and Amaymon

Find answers to difficult problems.
When faced with a problem that keeps circling in your mind, it is difficult to let go and allow answers to emerge from your subconscious. Myrmo can grant you the power to find the space to contemplate, but may also offer direct solutions. New ideas may come to mind in the days that follow, but you will certainly feel more peace, and the problem will not feel as immovable. Allow yourself to think creatively in the days that follow the ritual.

Myrmo is pronounced as MEER-MOW. MEER as in MEER. MOW as in MOW.

First summon Lucifer. Then summon Oriens. Then summon Paymon. Then summon Ariton. Then summon Amaymon, before proceeding to summon Myrmo.

The Pathworking of Myrmo

A young woman with black hair stands by a well.
Wine is poured over snail shells.
A pile of wet black rocks on a path through the forest.

Trapis

Under Oriens, Paymon, Ariton, and Amaymon

To be seen as innocent by all who hear you speak.

It has been said that no ritual needs repeating unless there is a change that calls for such repetition, but this power is an exception because it is an inevitability that the trust you exude will fade over several months. When you call on this power, Trapis will grant it immediately, and you will be seen as trustworthy. This only works for the spoken word, not for anything you write, so use this power wisely. If you wish to continue using the power, repeat it after five or six months, or if you notice a definite fading of the power. It can be used when you are guilty of something, to conceal your actions, or to appear as one who is beyond suspicion in all matters, which can have many benefits, such as covering up small errors of judgment.

Trapis is pronounced as TRAP-IS. TRAP as in TRAP. IS as in IS. (Note that IS sounds more like IZZ than ISS.)

First summon Lucifer. Then summon Oriens. Then summon Paymon. Then summon Ariton. Then summon Amaymon, before proceeding to summon Trapis.

The Pathworking of Trapis

Red sunrise catches the dew of a meadow.
An empty cornucopia woven from grass.
A wasteland scattered with white feathers and bloodied beaks.

Parelit

Under Oriens, Paymon, Ariton, and Amaymon

To compel somebody to decide swiftly and in your favour.
When you require a decision to be made in your favour, and at speed, call on Parelit to grant this power, and name the person or people who will make the decision. Use this when the urgent need is real and is not created merely out of impatience.

Parelit is pronounced as PA-RAY-LIT. PA as in PARDON. RAY as in RAY. LIT as in LIT.

First summon Lucifer. Then summon Oriens. Then summon Paymon. Then summon Ariton. Then summon Amaymon, before proceeding to summon Parelit.

The Pathworking of Parelit

Where two rivers meet, they turn to the colour of mud.
The body of a stag, rotting.
The moon rises, a yellow crescent over a plain of grey stone.

Obedemah

Under Oriens, Paymon, Ariton, and Amaymon

To protect your home and possessions.
It is wise to use this each time you move into a new dwelling, or if you are new to magick, as your first ritual. It will not prevent every accident, burglary or storm from harming all that you own, but it will make accidental loss or damage far less likely. What seems like a trivial power will appear more impressive when yours is the one house left standing after a storm.

Obedemah is pronounced as OB-ED-EM-AH. OB as in JOB. ED as in FED. EM as in EMBER. AH is the A sound in FATHER.

First summon Lucifer. Then summon Oriens. Then summon Paymon. Then summon Ariton. Then summon Amaymon, before proceeding to summon Obedemah.

The Pathworking of Obedemah

In the middle of a field, reeds surround a pond.
Beetles crawl over the freshly ploughed field.
You stand by a freshly felled tree, its green leaves dripping with blood.

Hasperim

Under Oriens, Paymon, Ariton, and Amaymon

Make a competitor suffer from a poor reputation.
In business, reputation is as important as the products you sell, and you can encourage the spread of mistrust and ill words regarding your competitor.

Hasperim is pronounced as HAS-PEAR-EEM. HAS as in HAS (where the S sounds more like Z.) PEAR as in PEAR. EEM as in SEEM.

First summon Lucifer. Then summon Oriens. Then summon Paymon. Then summon Ariton. Then summon Amaymon, before proceeding to summon Hasperim.

The Pathworking of Hasperim

A cave lit by a red flame the comes from a pool of black oil.
A young, naked woman, her hair sticky with wet blood.
At the entrance to the cave there is moonlight and the smell of grass.

Fasma

Under Oriens, Paymon, Ariton, and Amaymon

Cause somebody to be paranoid.
When paranoid, a person of great strength and wisdom will become weak and irrational. The potential of this power is clear. A person who becomes too paranoid can be a liability, so you may wish to summon Fasma once more, to lessen or remove the effect when sufficient damage has been done.

Fasma is pronounced as FAS-MAH. FAS as in FAST. MA as in MARTYR.

First summon Lucifer. Then summon Oriens. Then summon Paymon. Then summon Ariton. Then summon Amaymon, before proceeding to summon Fasma.

The Pathworking of Fasma

A field of poppies with snowy mountains in the distance.
Flies buzz around the corpse of a skinned rabbit.
A willow tree by a shallow river.

Nogah

Under Oriens, Paymon, Ariton, and Amaymon

Banish spirits that have been sent to torment you.
A power is no power at all unless you know how to use it, and most people who are attacked by magick never suspect they may be suffering at the hands of many creatures of spirit. It is also apparent that many people believe they are assailed by demons and other entities when they are under no such attack. This power will banish spirits that have been sent to work against you, but how can you know that is the case? I do not believe this should be performed every few months, to ensure spirits are banished, although some disagree and use the ritual in that way. I would only choose to summon this power if I noticed unusual sensations or omens that occurred on a frequent basis. If you suspect an attack, you can use the ritual to ensure your safety, but I urge you not to become too attached to the idea that you are under constant attack. It is all too common for those who work magick to assume, mistakenly, that others care to attack them. Banish only when required.

Nogah is pronounced as GNAW-GAR. GNAW as in GNAW. GAR as in GARDEN.

First summon Lucifer. Then summon Oriens. Then summon Paymon. Then summon Ariton. Then summon Amaymon, before proceeding to summon Nogah.

The Pathworking of Nogah

An endless field of grass.
The grass is singed black where molten gold has been poured into the soil.
You stand on a hilltop surrounded by burnt branches and blackened bones.

Ethanim

Under Oriens, Paymon, Ariton, and Amaymon

To find a stable job.
If you are seeking a new job, and one that will bring stability, call on the power of Ethanim. No guarantee can be made as to job satisfaction or the quality of the workplace, so use your discretion in selecting the correct opportunity.

Ethanim is pronounced as ETH-AN-EEM. ETH as in METHOD. AN as in CAN. EEM as in SEEM.

First summon Lucifer. Then summon Oriens. Then summon Paymon. Then summon Ariton. Then summon Amaymon, before proceeding to summon Ethanim.

The Pathworking of Ethanim

A crescent moon in the evening sky.
A human spine, fresh and bloody, broken in two.
You stand in a flooded field, water stretching to the horizon.

Melabed

Under Oriens, Paymon, Ariton, and Amaymon

To request a growth in your income.
This power enables your career or work to become more profitable in many imaginative and unexpected ways. When you request more income, you may be required to do more work in order to obtain that income. Be willing to do the extra work if new opportunities arrive. You will never be given more work than you can cope with because Melabed's power is creative but gentle.

Melabed is pronounced as MEL-AB-ED. MEL as in MELT. AB as in DAB. ED as in BED.

First summon Lucifer. Then summon Oriens. Then summon Paymon. Then summon Ariton. Then summon Amaymon, before proceeding to summon Melabed.

The Pathworking of Melabed

In the rain, the remains of a bonfire, smoking.
Wine poured over human bones.
A wasteland of scorched tree stumps and at your feet a blackened sword.

Apolion

Under Oriens, Paymon, Ariton, and Amaymon

Discover somebody's true thoughts.

People rarely say what they mean, and most of the time this doesn't matter, but if you feel the need to know what somebody believes about you or a situation you are connected to, summon Apolion. You will become aware of the person's true thoughts each time they communicate with you, either as they speak, or as you read what they have written to you. It may take a few days to develop the skill of listening or reading while also sensing the true thoughts behind what is spoken or written.

Apolion is pronounced as APP-AWE-LEE-ORN. APP as in APPLY. AWE as in AWE. LEE as in LEEK. ORN as in TORN. Some prefer APP-OLL-EE-ON, with APP as in APPLY, OLL as in DOLL, EE as in SEE and ON as in ON.

First summon Lucifer. Then summon Oriens. Then summon Paymon. Then summon Ariton. Then summon Amaymon, before proceeding to summon Apolion.

The Pathworking of Apolion

A black horse galloping on the horizon.
A motionless man in flames, feeling no pain.
At the edge of a foul, reeking pond, blue flames flicker from the mud.

Asturel

Under Oriens, Paymon, Ariton, and Amaymon

To make you calm and clear-minded when pressured by intense questioning.
If you know you are about to be interviewed, accused, appear in court or be questioned in any other aggressive manner, whether guilty or not, this is a power you should summon. Asturel will help you to remain calm, and the right answers will often arise as you speak.

Asturel is pronounced as ARE-STEW-RAIL. ARE as in ARE. STEW as in STEW. RAIL as in RAIL.

First summon Lucifer. Then summon Oriens. Then summon Paymon. Then summon Ariton. Then summon Amaymon, before proceeding to summon Asturel.

The Pathworking of Asturel

A fallow field, hard with winter frost.
A man kneels, and arrow lodged in the back of his neck.
You stand in the snow at the base of a white, chalky cliff.

Hagrion

Under Oriens, Paymon, Ariton and Amaymon

To break a known curse, even when somebody has made a link to you.

In some magickal traditions, your attacker may obtain a link to you, such as a personal possession or a strand of your hair. While such magick is often weak, that is not always the case, and if it has been well-crafted, the link makes it more powerful. If you suspect such a curse is in place, Hagrion will remove it. It is said elsewhere that detecting an attack can be difficult, or a matter of guesswork, but if you feel or suspect an attack, summon Hagrion and ask that all curses against you be broken. Even if somebody has a link to you, it will be disconnected and will cause no more trouble. You may also get a very clear impression of the person who has cursed you, but this is not always the case.

Hagrion is pronounced as HAG-REE-ON. HAG as in HAG. REE as in REED. ON as in ON.

First summon Lucifer. Then summon Oriens. Then summon Paymon. Then summon Ariton. Then summon Amaymon, before proceeding to summon Hagrion.

The Pathworking of Hagrion

The scorched remains of a forest at dawn.
A breeze that smells of raw fish, salt, and seaweed.
A circle of saplings by the entrance to a cave.

Liriol

Under Oriens, Paymon, Ariton, and Amaymon

To bind a person, so they are unable to work against you.
Binding is a lesser form of cursing, where you do no harm, but
you ensure the person you name can cause you no harm, either
through their actions and words or through magick. Binding is
found throughout magick but is often complex and short-term.
Liriol grants you a formidable method of binding that will be
ongoing.

Liriol is pronounced as LEE-REE-ALL. LEE is the LEE sound
in LEAN or LEAP. REE as in REED. ALL as in ALL.

First summon Lucifer. Then summon Oriens. Then summon
Paymon. Then summon Ariton. Then summon Amaymon,
before proceeding to summon Liriol.

The Pathworking of Liriol

In the meadow, maggots ooze from the remains of a hare.
The body of a dead snake, its eyes bloody.
Three black standing stones, taller than a person, lodged in
white sand by a frozen lake.

Asorega

Under Oriens, Paymon, Ariton, and Amaymon

Discover the true name of somebody who works against you in secret.

It is not uncommon to know the pseudonym of an enemy while being unaware of their true identity. This is not a product of the internet age, although it is probably more common now than it has been before. If you know of somebody who maligns you in a public or online arena, but you know they are using a false name, this summoning will lead you to perceive the true name of that person. You may be led to a trail of evidence, or you may become aware of the person directly because they are already known to you. When the realisation hits you, it will be unmistakable. This power only works if the person in question is actively working against you in some way, so if you have made an error of judgement and they are harmless, nothing will be revealed.

Asorega is pronounced as AS-OAR-AY-GORE. AS as in AS (with more of a Z sound than and S.) OAR as in BOAR. AY as in PAY. GORE as in GORE.

First summon Lucifer. Then summon Oriens. Then summon Paymon. Then summon Ariton. Then summon Amaymon, before proceeding to summon Asorega.

The Pathworking of Asorega

A black tower on a hillside.
Hailstone falls in the bright green grass.
A smashed pomegranate mixed with human blood.
The bodies of black birds float down a muddy river, in a flat land of wet, brown earth.

Ragaras

Under Oriens, Paymon, Ariton, and Amaymon

To make somebody lose their source of wealth.
There are thousands of ways to become wealthy, and although many people are born into money, and others earn it through hard work, some come by wealth through good timing or great ideas. Whatever the source of wealth, you can separate a named individual from that source. It does not mean they will lose all that they have (although they may), but it does mean they will have no means to make money unless they acquire a new set of skills and change their life. The disruption is such that most people will suffer greatly before establishing any degree of recovery.

Ragaras is pronounced as RAG-ARE-AS. RAG as in RAG. ARE as in ARE. AS as in AS (with the S sounding more like the Z sound.)

First summon Lucifer. Then summon Oriens. Then summon Paymon. Then summon Ariton. Then summon Amaymon, before proceeding to summon Ragaras.

The Pathworking of Ragaras

In the forest, smoke and sunlight.
In a glade the bloodied horns of a stag.
At the edge of the forest, white flowers and mushrooms grow around a golden dagger.

Ilekal

Under Oriens, Paymon, Ariton, and Amaymon

Learn to perceive when people are speaking the truth.
This power gives you the ability to detect liars. As with many of these rituals it does not work for the written word, or if you a speaking over a phone or screen, but it works extremely well when you speak in person. Summon Ilekal and ask for this power and it will develop within you. If there is a time when you need to know if a particular person is lying or bending the truth you can summon Ilekal once more and ask for your perception to be focussed on that individual. You will find it quite easy to sense when you are being lied to.

Ilekal is pronounced as ILL-ECK-AL. ILL as in PILL. ECK as in NECK. AL as in BALANCE.

First summon Lucifer. Then summon Oriens. Then summon Paymon. Then summon Ariton. Then summon Amaymon, before proceeding to summon Ilekal.

The Pathworking of Ilekal

By the edge of a river the bodies of dead rats.
A ceramic pot of boiling oil.
You stand on black rock at the edge of an immense white waterfall, overlooking a flooded valley.

Sarasim

Under Oriens, Paymon, Ariton, and Amaymon

To cause somebody to suffer accidental injury.
It is difficult to control the extent to which somebody may be injured, but do not assume that an accident will be as mild as a paper cut or as extreme as death. When you give a name to Sarasim, you will bring an accidental injury to that person, and it will be at a level that is more than an inconvenience. It could also be quite life-changing, so only summon this power if you are willing to accept the potential range of its effect without guilt or regret.

Sarasim is pronounced as SA-RAISE-EEM. SA as in the first part of SAD. RAISE as in RAISE. EEM as in SEEM.

First summon Lucifer. Then summon Oriens. Then summon Paymon. Then summon Ariton. Then summon Amaymon, before proceeding to summon Sarasim.

The Pathworking of Sarasim

A black dog stands by the entrance to a cave.
Within a cave flames rise from a pool of oil.
The walls of the cave are veined with silver and gold.

Sigis

Under Oriens, Paymon, Ariton, and Amaymon

Protect those that you care about.

This power is one of general protection for those that you love. Rituals that command powers of a general nature are often weak because they attempt to control too much. This power works because Sigis is aware of what would cause you pain, and is able to prevent those situations. Where they cannot be stopped, they will be lessened. The ritual does not need be to repeated unless there is a new addition to your family, your group of friends, or those you choose to protect.

Sigis is pronounced as SIEGE-ISS. SIEGE as in SIEGE. ISS as in HISS.

First summon Lucifer. Then summon Oriens. Then summon Paymon. Then summon Ariton. Then summon Amaymon, before proceeding to summon Sigis.

The Pathworking of Sigis

Grey sky over a lake of blood at dawn.
A fallen tree in an empty field with the full moon in a blue sky.
A black dog stands over the skeleton of a horse

Laralos

Under Oriens, Paymon, Ariton, and Amaymon

To make two people feel disgusted with each other.
This power can be used to make a couple suffer and possibly separate, but can also be used to create problems with friends, family members, and even business associates. Give the names of the two people to Laralos.

Laralos is pronounced as LAR-AL-OSS. LAR as in LARGE. AL as in BALANCE. OSS as in TOSS.

First summon Lucifer. Then summon Oriens. Then summon Paymon. Then summon Ariton. Then summon Amaymon, before proceeding to summon Laralos.

The Pathworking of Laralos

An apple tree overladen with fruit.
Scorched human hair on a freshly dug grave.
You stand on a floor of black rock encircled by mossy cliffs.

Ipakol

Under Oriens, Paymon, Ariton, and Amaymon

To remove the will to curse.
If you know somebody is cursing you or others, and you wish to stop them rather than deflect or counter those curses, you can remove that person's will to curse. Summon Ipakol and name the person, asking that they lose the will to curse.

Ipakol is pronounced as EEP-ACK-ALL. EEP as in JEEP. ACK as in JACK. ALL as in ALL.

First summon Lucifer. Then summon Oriens. Then summon Paymon. Then summon Ariton. Then summon Amaymon, before proceeding to summon Ipakol.

<u>The Pathworking of Ipakol</u>

Beyond the meadows, snowy mountains at dawn.
Wheat trampled underfoot.
You stand at the edge of a blue lake surrounded by snowy mountains.

Balabos

Under Oriens, Paymon, Ariton, and Amaymon

Detect the intentions of an enemy or competitor.
To succeed when you are set against a strong enemy or competitor, it helps to know what they are planning to do next. By summoning Balabos, you may learn of their plans because they become loose of tongue, or because you gain intuition about what is coming next. With this knowledge, you can act with more wisdom and creativity.

Balabos is pronounced as BALA-BOSS. BALA as in BALANCE. BOSS as in BOSS.

First summon Lucifer. Then summon Oriens. Then summon Paymon. Then summon Ariton. Then summon Amaymon, before proceeding to summon Balabos.

The Pathworking of Balabos

A full moon in the sunset.
An old man in filthy robes points at the moon.
A black mountainside glowing with a river of smoking lava.

Nolom

Under Oriens, Paymon, Ariton, and Amaymon

Cause somebody to doubt their magickal abilities.
Some people make public boasts about their use of magick, and even if they use a fake name to do so, they have named themselves, so you can summon Nolom to bring doubt. When somebody who is powerful with magick becomes filled with doubt, they perform less magick, and the magick they have performed is less likely to work. This is an excellent way to disarm an experienced occultist.

Nolom is pronounced as GNAW-LOAM. GNAW as in GNAW. LOAM as in LOAM.

First summon Lucifer. Then summon Oriens. Then summon Paymon. Then summon Ariton. Then summon Amaymon, before proceeding to summon Nolom.

The Pathworking of Nolom

Dead rats rotting in a moonlit forest.
Two children kneel before a standing stone.
A treeless space within the forest with a dry riverbed.

Amillis

Under Oriens, Paymon, Ariton, and Amaymon

Cause arguments and mistrust within a group.
Groups appear powerful but are often weaker than individuals because many intentions are pulling in different directions, and there are always those who would undermine and usurp the leaders. Summon Amillis and ask for arguments and mistrust to develop within a group and you will see the effects emerging. Some groups are shattered or damaged irreparably in a short time.

Amillis is pronounced as AM-EE-LIS. AM as in AM. EE as in SEE. LIS as in LIST, where the S sounds like SSS more than Z.

First summon Lucifer. Then summon Oriens. Then summon Paymon. Then summon Ariton. Then summon Amaymon, before proceeding to summon Amillis.

The Pathworking of Amillis

A barren land of dry earth.
Horse hoofprints in the clay.
A naked pregnant woman stands by an open grave.
A slab of black stone in a garden of yellow roses.

The Demon Servants of Astaroth and Asmodi

To summon the Demon Servants of Astaroth and Asmodi, you must first summon Lucifer and ask Lucifer to grant you the power to summon the named Demon Dukes and their Demon Servant.

If you were summoning Dagulez, you might say, 'Lucifer, I ask that you allow me to summon Astaroth, Asmodi, and Dagulez.' You would then summon Astaroth and say, 'Astaroth, I ask that you allow me to summon Dagulez.' You would then use the Pathworking to summon Asmodi, and you would say, 'Asmodi, I ask that you allow me to summon Dagulez.' You would then summon Dagulez, and make your request directly to Dagulez. This process is the same for all the Demon Servants of Astaroth and Asmodi that follow in this section.

Lagiros

Under Astaroth and Asmodi

To fill somebody with uncontrollable anger.
This is a risky strategy and one that should be used with great caution if you cross the path of this person. You may also want to consider the moral implications because uncontrollable anger could lead the person you name to strike out against those you love. The purpose of the ritual is to make the person you name become so angry that they make mistakes, ruin relationships, or get into trouble that they can't handle.

Lagiros is pronounced as LAG-EE-ROSS. LAG as in FLAG. EE as in SEE. ROSS as in CROSS.

First summon Lucifer. Then summon Astaroth. Then summon Asmodi, before proceeding to summon Lagiros.

The Pathworking of Lagiros

Two dead brown fish float on the surface of a pond.
Sticks tied in a bundle with red thread.
Three cracked boulders in a meadow flattened by rain.

Ugalis

Under Astaroth and Asmodi

To attract another through an appearance of calm power.
Not everybody is attracted by power, but many are, and if you sense that somebody may find this quality attractive, summon Ugalis. You will be granted the power to appear calm and powerful, and this requires no effort on your part, but you may find that you begin to feel calmer and more powerful in the coming weeks.

Ugalis is pronounced as OO-GAL-EASE. OO as in POOL. GAL as in GALANT. EASE as in EASE.

First summon Lucifer. Then summon Astaroth. Then summon Asmodi, before proceeding to summon Ugalis.

The Pathworking of Ugalis

Mist rises from a swamp at sunset.
Bird feathers and white human teeth shine in the moonlight.
The sun rises as a white circle over pale blue mountains.

Dagulez

Under Astaroth and Asmodi

To appear younger.
It is not always wise to appear younger, as it can make you look more foolish, depending upon your age. If you have reached an age where you wish to look young, this power will enable your true health to show while generating a degree of illusion that can make you appear younger. The ritual does not need to be repeated unless you suffer from a long illness as that can have the effect of making you appear older.

Dagulez is pronounced as DAR-GOO-LEZ. DAR as in DARK. GOO as in GOO (rhymes with DO.) LEZ as in the first part of LESBIAN, where LES sounds like LEZ.

First summon Lucifer. Then summon Astaroth. Then summon Asmodi, before proceeding to summon Dagulez.

The Pathworking of Dagulez

A waterfall stained with blood.
Worms dying in the sun as they crawl from the soil.
In the middle of a ploughed field a pear tree surrounded by its fallen fruit.

Bialod

Under Astaroth and Asmodi

To tempt somebody into being disloyal.
This power can be used to make somebody sexually disloyal to their partner. The power, though, is not there to help you win somebody from another, but to cause disruption between a couple. It does so by making the one you name burn with the desire to be disloyal. If you are already in a situation where you might be the one they choose for their misdemeanour, it can work in your favour, but you cannot rely on this. If you are aiming to make the couple separate, you can summon Bialod twice, once for each person, so that both are tempted into disloyalty. In most cases, this has the potential to bring the relationship to an end.

Bialod is pronounced as BEE-AL-ORD. BEE as in BEE. AL as in BALANCE. ORD as in LORD.

First summon Lucifer. Then summon Astaroth. Then summon Asmodi, before proceeding to summon Bialod.

The Pathworking of Bialod

Hail stones from a white, featureless sky.
A frozen lake, smeared with bloody footprints.
A wheat field flattened by hail and snow.

Ranar

Under Astaroth and Asmodi

Speak with clarity and confidence.
This power is not for specific occasions but is used to help you develop the skill of speaking more clearly and without hesitation so that you appear confident.

Ranar is pronounced as RAN-ARE. RAN as in RAN. ARE as in ARE.

First summon Lucifer. Then summon Astaroth. Then summon Asmodi, before proceeding to summon Ranar.

The Pathworking of Ranar

A white river between black mountains.
A pale boy offers a shining dagger.
A three-way crossroads in the forest, with a storm overhead.

Buriub

Under Astaroth and Asmodi

To influence through the calm power of your voice.
Summon Buriub to give you the power to influence, and focus on keeping a calm tone in your voice when you aim to convince. This power develops over time but is one of the most powerful granted by the entire legion of demons if used wisely.

Buriub is pronounced as BOO-REE-UB. BOO as in BOON. REE as in REED. UB as in STUB.

First summon Lucifer. Then summon Astaroth. Then summon Asmodi, before proceeding to summon Buriub.

<u>The Pathworking of Buriub</u>

A misty valley with a circle of standing stones.
A silver spear broken in two.
A golden key on a slab of obsidian.

Nimalon

Under Astaroth and Asmodi

Make a competitor waste money.
This power can be used against anybody you feel to be a competitor, whether that is in sport, business or your personal life, and it causes them to be utterly reckless with money. This can have the effect of making the person seem bright and attractive to others for a short while, as excessive spending can seem exciting and generous, but given time it will be extremely damaging.

Nimalon is pronounced as KNEE-MAL-ON. KNEE as in KNEE. MAL as in MALADY. ON as in ON.

First summon Lucifer. Then summon Astaroth. Then summon Asmodi, before proceeding to summon Nimalon.

The Pathworking of Nimalon

Moonlight on a frosted field.
A red sunrise through the pale, misty sky.
The smoking remains of a burned tree float down a muddy river.

Bagalon

Under Astaroth and Asmodi

To make somebody feel in awe of you.
Making another person feel awe for you can give you the ability to ask for many things from them. It can also make some people resent you because being awed by you goes against their beliefs or expected feelings, so use your judgement when calling for this power. If it becomes a problem, you can summon the demon and ask for the sense of awe to fade.

Bagalon is pronounced as BAG-ARE-LAWN. BAG as in BAG. ARE as in ARE. LAWN as in LAWN.

First summon Lucifer. Then summon Astaroth. Then summon Asmodi, before proceeding to summon Bagalon.

The Pathworking of Bagalon

Ash and white blossom drift on the grey rock.
On a flat granite hilltop, three bonfires rage.

Anamalon

Under Astaroth and Asmodi

To arouse sexual thoughts in others when you speak.
You do not want everybody to have sexual thoughts when you speak, so aim this ritual at an individual or a small number of named individuals. When you subsequently talk, whatever the subject matter, sexual thoughts will occur in the other person or people, possibly causing arousal. This may lead to nothing more than flirting but it can spice up otherwise dull occasions and can bring more opportunities for starting relationships.

Anamalon is pronounced as AN-AM-ARE-LAWN. AN as in AN. AM as in AM. ARE as in ARE. LAWN as in LAWN.

First summon Lucifer. Then summon Astaroth. Then summon Asmodi, before proceeding to summon Anamalon.

The Pathworking of Anamalon

At sunrise, a noose hangs from an autumnal tree.
The skeletons of birds in the fallen red leaves.
A scattering of emeralds on the soil of the forest floor.

Sagarez

Under Astaroth and Asmodi

To radiate sexual potency through your gaze.
Ask the demon to give you the power as described, and know the power will be with you for many months, or even longer. It is not something that wears off unless you stop using it. When you want to use the power, look into the eyes of somebody you find attractive. Hold their gaze for a moment and feel your sexual potency. If the person is repulsed by you, or even disinterested, they will sense your potency and will avert their gaze. This may seem disappointing, but it is an excellent technique to help you avoid wasting time on somebody who will not respond to your sexual energy. If you hold somebody's gaze and if they feel any attraction toward you at all, they will sense your potency and may become open to being with you. You will almost certainly see this in their eyes. You will then need to act on this in some way, probably by starting a conversation. Nobody likes a creepy person who stares at people in an attempt to look alluring, so use this without being aggressive or too obvious.

Sagarez is pronounced as SAG-ARE-EZZ. SAG as in SAG. ARE as in ARE. EZZ as in FEZZ.

First summon Lucifer. Then summon Astaroth. Then summon Asmodi, before proceeding to summon Sagarez.

The Pathworking of Sagarez

Calm ocean water at sunset.
Three shattered skulls by a rockpool.
You stand at the dripping edge of a blue-white glacier, between black mountains.

The Demon Servants of Asmodi and Magoth

To summon the Demon Servants of Asmodi and Magoth, you must first summon Lucifer and ask Lucifer to grant you the power to summon the named Demon Dukes and their Demon Servant.

If you were summoning Kela, you might say, 'Lucifer, I ask that you allow me to summon Asmodi, Magoth, and Kela.' You would then summon Asmodi and say, 'Asmodi, I ask that you allow me to summon Kela.' You would then summon Magoth, and you would say, 'Magoth, I ask that you allow me to summon Kela.' You would then summon Kela, and make your request directly to Kela. This process is the same for all the Demon Servants of Asmodi and Magoth that follow in this section.

Kela

Under Asmodi and Magoth

To fill somebody with self-loathing.
As with many of the powers in this book, it can be used for revenge and punishment, or to gain a strategic advantage over an enemy or competitor.

Kela is pronounced as KEY-LA. KEY as in KEY. LA as in LARD.

First summon Lucifer. Then summon Asmodi. Then summon Magoth, before proceeding to summon Kela.

The Pathworking of Kela

A lightning storm over the ocean.
A rusted knife in the grass, its tip wet with blood.
A noose hangs from a dead tree in a field of bright green grass.

Diopes

Under Asmodi and Magoth

Request money for a specific purpose.
Financial magick is often constrained by many external factors, which is why it can often disappoint, even though it is by far the most attractive magick to the beginner. The power presented here is effective when you request money for a specific purpose that is not too far removed from your normal life. You can request a sum to help you when you need it, but if you ask for the money to buy a house, you are only fooling yourself. Look to your immediate needs. There may be something you desire to own, a debt you wish to settle, or merely a sense of peace that more money would bring. If you can name the purpose, and the amount you need, the magick can work. Avoid setting a time limit, even within your own mind, and do not predict how or where the money will come from. Expect, but do not demand, and the ritual will satisfy your needs.

Diopes is pronounced as DEE-OPE-ESS. DEE as in DEEP. OPE as in HOPE. ESS as in PRESS.

First summon Lucifer. Then summon Asmodi. Then summon Magoth, before proceeding to summon Diopes.

The Pathworking of Diopes

Lightning from a blue sky, over a field of wheat.
Wet green footprints through frosted grass.
You stand at the base of a small hill that is surrounded by a wall of black bricks.

Magyros

Under Asmodi and Magoth

To become a well of new ideas with financial potential.
Whether you are working in business, as a freelancer, or trying to bring benefit to a company you work for, you need ideas with financial potential. Become known for this skill, and you will be sought out by those who need you. If you work for yourself, the skill will make you able to find the best ideas much faster.

Magyros is pronounced as MAG-EAR-OSS. MAG as in MAGAZINE. EAR as in EAR. OSS as in TOSS.

First summon Lucifer. Then summon Asmodi. Then summon Magoth, before proceeding to summon Magyros.

The Pathworking of Magyros

A garden filled with white flowers.
Smoke leaking from a broken sphere of white rock.
A burned hillside of black grass and ash, with a raven atop a white standing stone.

Lamargos

Under Asmodi and Magoth

To make a lover more experimental and disinhibited.
Use this ritual to make a named lover, who already knows and trusts you, to become more exciting and interesting during sex. Do not make any suggestions yourself, or urge any experimentation as this seems to break the spell. Instead, wait for your partner to make a move in a new direction. Perform this with caution because your partner may ask for experiences that you are not willing to be a part of.

Lamargos is pronounced as LAMB-ARE-GOSS. LAMB as in LAMB. ARE as in ARE. GOSS as in GOSSAMER.

First summon Lucifer. Then summon Asmodi. Then summon Magoth, before proceeding to summon Lamargos.

The Pathworking of Lamargos

A hammer of gold on a muddy riverbank.
A tree stump crawling with ants, in a waterlogged field.

Disolel

Under Asmodi and Magoth

To cause minor ailments to occur continually.
Minor ailments are anything but minor when they occur continuously. If your enemy catches one cold or sickness after another, with each illness overlapping, it is impossible to regain the strength to be whole. This can punish an enemy or make you have the advantage in competitive situations.

Disolel is pronounced as DIS-AWE-LELL. DIS as in DISTANT. AWE as in AWE. LELL as in PARALLEL.

First summon Lucifer. Then summon Asmodi. Then summon Magoth, before proceeding to summon Disolel.

The Pathworking of Disolel

A rocky hilltop in blue morning twilight.
Snow falling on wet, black rock, where it freezes.
A circle of boulders on a hilltop surrounded by black mountains.

The Demon Servants of Amaymon and Ariton

To summon the Demon Servants of Amaymon and Ariton, you must first summon Lucifer and ask Lucifer to grant you the power to summon the named Demon Dukes and their Demon Servant.

If you were summoning Irasomin, you might say, 'Lucifer, I ask that you allow me to summon Amaymon, Ariton, and Irasomin.' You would then summon Amaymon and say, 'Amaymon, I ask that you allow me to summon Irasomin.' You would then summon Ariton, and you would say, 'Ariton, I ask that you allow me to summon Irasomin.' You would then summon Irasomin, and make your request directly to Irasomin. This process is the same for all the Demon Servants of Amaymon and Ariton that follow in this section.

Harog

Under Amaymon and Ariton

To protect against accidents.
This is a power of general protection that can be performed at any time, to give ongoing security that helps you avoid accidents. It can also be used when you know you are entering a situation that is less stable or predictable than usual, to ensure your safety.

Harog is pronounced as HAR-AUG. HAR as in HARD. AUG as in AUGUST.

First summon Lucifer. Then summon Amaymon. Then summon Ariton, before proceeding to summon Harog.

The Pathworking of Harog

An apple orchard strewn with rotten fruit.
A young boy in black sits at the foot of a dead tree.
You stand in a circle of young white trees, their leaves rippling in the breeze.

Agebol

Under Amaymon and Ariton

To protect against attack when traveling.
The most inconvenient time to be attacked, and often the most common, is when you are travelling. Attacks may be as mild as pickpocketing (which can ruin several days of your travels), or they can be violent and extremely dangerous. Before you travel, perform this ritual and ask that the demon protects you against attack during your travels.

Agebol is pronounced as AG-AY-BALL. AG as in STAG. AY as in PAY. BALL as in BALL.

First summon Lucifer. Then summon Amaymon. Then summon Ariton, before proceeding to summon Agebol.

The Pathworking of Agebol

Rotten reeds at the edge of a frozen lake.
The scattered, broken bones of a human leg on wet earth.
Three rusted daggers in the snow.
You stand by an icy cliff next to the clean white bones of a dead dog.

Rigolen

Under Amaymon and Ariton

To cause a person to feel anxious about a situation.
When you know somebody is going to be in a specific situation, such as a meeting, job interview, public appearance, or competition, you can make them feel anxious. The level of anxiety will be such that they underperform or are unable to continue with the performance. You can perform this ritual immediately before the moment in question if you have no time to spare, but if you can plan ahead, perform it at least a week before the event, so there is time for the anxiety and apprehension to build.

Rigolen is pronounced as RIG-OW-LEN. RIG as in RIGGING. OW as in SHOW. LEN as in LEND.

First summon Lucifer. Then summon Amaymon. Then summon Ariton, before proceeding to summon Rigolen.

The Pathworking of Rigolen

A green, spring forest shimmers in a strong breeze.
The grass is grey and white.
Honey leaks from the remains of a broken silver jar.
The trees are leafless in the sickly yellow light of sunset.

Irasomin

Under Amaymon and Ariton

Recover emotionally from a setback.
If you have experienced a setback in any area of life, recover from it emotionally, by summoning this demon and allowing the power to heal the moment. The sooner you can move on, the lesser the setback becomes.

Irasomin is pronounced as EAR-ASS-OWE-MEAN. EAR as in EAR. ASS as in PASS. OWE as in OWE. MEAN as in MEAN.

First summon Lucifer. Then summon Amaymon. Then summon Ariton, before proceeding to summon Irasomin.

The Pathworking of Irasomin

Flames rise from a rock on the beach, at night.
The horns of a bull on a slab of granite.

Elafon

Under Amaymon and Ariton

Find balance between self-esteem and ego.
Magick that works on the self can be more powerful than any magick that seeks an external result. The ego is not something you need to conquer because without an ego you wouldn't get out of bed, but it needs to be balanced against a healthy sense of self-esteem. This power will help you achieve self-esteem without becoming egotistical. Low self-esteem or an overblown ego are barriers to success, and finding this balance, although not a spectacular power, can attract spectacular results.

Elafon is pronounced as ELL-AFF-AWN. ELL as in TELL. AFF as in STAFF. AWN as in LAWN.

First summon Lucifer. Then summon Amaymon. Then summon Ariton, before proceeding to summon Elafon.

The Pathworking of Elafon

A meadow of grass and flowers, and on the horizon a forest in flames.
Sapphires and a silver key on a slab of obsidian.

The Demon Servants of Astaroth

To summon the Demon Servants of Astaroth, you must first summon Lucifer and ask Lucifer to grant you the power to summon the named Demon Duke and the Demon Servant.

If you were summoning Ombalafa, you might say, 'Lucifer, I ask that you allow me to summon Astaroth and Ombalafa.' You would then summon Astaroth and say, 'Astaroth, I ask that you allow me to summon Ombalafa.' You would then summon Ombalafa, and make your request directly to Ombalafa. This process is the same for all the Demon Servants of Astaroth that follow in this section.

Iromenis

Under Astaroth

For an increase in luck when gambling.
When you win at gambling, it brings an intense rush of pleasure. The ritual does not improve your skills, for games that involve skill as well as chance, but improves your fortune. Improved fortune does not guarantee a win, but if you are going to gamble, you would be a fool to absent magick from your activity.

Bring financial loss to those who build their success on your work, ideas or reputation.
When somebody has built their business by using your abilities, reputation, or even your name, you may wish them great harm. If you do wish to cause them harm for leeching off you, this power will bring many instances of damaging financial loss.

Iromenis is pronounced as EAR-OWE-MEN-ISS. EAR as in EAR. OWE as in OWE. MEN as in MEN. ISS as in MISS.

First summon Lucifer. Then summon Astaroth. Proceed to summon Iromenis.

The Pathworking of Iromenis

A black dog stands by an empty grave.
From the edge of the lake you see an island of green trees.

Apormanos

Under Astaroth

Discover the depths of your sexuality.
Not to be used merely because you are bored with your sex life, but when you are committed to seeing how deep and rich your sexuality may be, this power will open you to many tastes, desires, and impulses you have previously suppressed. It does not change you in a way that is disagreeable but opens you to desires you know are a part of you. It will not grant you the ability to satisfy those desires automatically, so it may take work on your part to find partners who will agree to work with your newly expanded sexuality. Some sensations are likely during the ritual, with revelations occurring in the weeks that follow.

To increase chance meetings that lead to sexual and emotional attraction.
This is a power that makes you more likely to meet somebody that you could have a relationship with, or at least have sex with. For online dating, it has no known effect. It works by making you more likely to meet people at social occasions, and they will be people who have the potential to become lovers or partners.

Apormanos is pronounced as APP-OAR-MAN-OSS. APP as in APPLY. OAR as in BOAR. MAN as in MAN. OSS as in TOSS.

First summon Lucifer. Then summon Astaroth. Proceed to summon Apormanos.

The Pathworking of Apormanos

Mist rises from a swamp at dawn.
Lava flows red down the side of many black mountains.
Standing in ashes, a yellow flower blooms at dusk.

Ombalafa

Under Astaroth

Compel somebody to feel intense remorse for their actions.
This does not appear to be the most intense form of revenge, but you may find great satisfaction when somebody breaks down before you, apologising for the ways they have wronged you. If somebody has previously defended their actions, they will instead become remorseful.

Make a competitor face unexpected disruption during a key business opportunity.
Perform this ritual when you know a competitor is involved in an opportunity that goes beyond the daily running of the business. If they are performing a presentation, hosting an event or making a deal, and you know about it, perform this ritual and ask the demon to bring disruption to your competitor's business life.

Ombalafa is pronounced as ORM-BAR-LAR-FAR. ORM as in DORM (rhymes with WARM). BAR as in BARD. LAR as in LARD. FAR as in FAR.

First summon Lucifer. Then summon Astaroth. Proceed to summon Ombalafa.

The Pathworking of Ombalafa

By the edge of a river snails leave silver trails on the ground.
A goat suckles on a naked, kneeling woman.
A broken crown of silver in the mud of the river.

Kataron

Under Astaroth

To improve artistry, craftworking, or creative expression.
If you work with arts or crafts, Kataron will improve your
ability to express yourself through such work.

Cause communication to be clear and honest.
The power should be directed at a single individual with
whom you wish to establish clear and honest communication.
This can establish a new relationship or repair one that is
damaged.

Kataron is pronounced as CAR-TA-RAWN. CAR as in CART.
TA as in TAP. RAWN as in DRAWN.

First summon Lucifer. Then summon Astaroth. Proceed to
summon Kataron.

The Pathworking of Kataron

Two dead silvery fish float on the surface of a pond.
Sticks tied in a bundle with red thread.
You stand atop a grassy hill, looking down at a forested valley
in flames.

Iloson

Under Astaroth

Become skilled at listening.
Being a good listener is not about being a shoulder to cry on, but means you are able to hear what the other person is saying, rather than planning your own words. By listening in this way, you become a more skilled communicator and negotiator.

To take the energy and vitality of another during sex.
If you are in a position to have sex with somebody, taking their energy would be a vampiric betrayal of trust. Although that power is possible, the real purpose of this is to use your sexual experience to drain the energy of a third party who is not even present. An unusual power, this enables you to focus on the third person, during sexual intercourse, and know that you are taking their energy, becoming stronger, and that they are being weakened. This is a strange and rarely used power, but the book would have been incomplete if it had not been listed. You do not need to tell your partner what you are doing. Perform the ritual as close to the sexual intercourse as you can, and no more than a day before.

Iloson is pronounced as EEL-AWE-SUN. EEL as in PEEL. AWE as in AWE. SUN as in SUNDAY.

First summon Lucifer. Then summon Astaroth. Proceed to summon Iloson.

The Pathworking of Iloson

A thunderstorm over the ocean.
A rusted knife on the sand.
A clear evening sky with a crescent moon over the calm ocean.

Kalotes

Under Astaroth

Learn fast and easily.
This power is not about skills but enables academic learning to be much easier. You can use it before a course begins, or when you are faced with a particular challenge.

Cause somebody to have sexual dreams about you.
Name the person you wish to affect. The result may or may not be obvious, and alone it can be useless, but used in conjunction with other rituals it can improve your chances of achieving your objective. You can even use this against an enemy to bring confusion and weakness.

Kalotes is pronounced as CAL-ORT-EZZ. CAL as in CALORIE. ORT as in FORT. EZZ as in FEZZ.

First summon Lucifer. Then summon Astaroth. Proceed to summon Kalotes.

The Pathworking of Kalotes

A pear orchard strewn with rotten fruit and flies.
A purple velvet cloak trampled into the mud.
A field of grass and blue flowers under a white, cloudy sky.

Golog

Under Astaroth

To be seen as an authority.
You can use this power to be seen as an authority, but you need to name the area in which you wish to be seen as an authority. If you are an author of books about birds, then you wish to be seen as an expert on birds. It does not make you appear authoritative about everything, but as an authority or expert on a specific subject. All who see you or your work will perceive you to be an authority on that subject, so you do not need to name anybody else in the ritual.

To improve your reputation amongst all who speak of you.
You can use this at any time, but you will reap the most benefit if you perform it during times of change, or when you know people will be talking about you. The power makes people who are critical of you quieter and brings greater enthusiasm and verbosity to those who admire you.

Golog is pronounced as GOAL-OG. GOAL as in GOAL. OG as in FOG.

First summon Lucifer. Then summon Astaroth. Proceed to summon Golog.

The Pathworking of Golog

In the forest, smoke and sunlight.
In a glade, the bloodied horns of a stag.
At the edge of the forest the grassy ground is marshy.
A full moon over the flooded lands, trees and branches floating in the water.

The Demon Servants of Asmodi

To summon the Demon Servants of Asmodi, you must first summon Lucifer and ask Lucifer to grant you the power to summon the named Demon Duke and the Demon Servant.

   If you were summoning Gillamon, you might say, 'Lucifer, I ask that you allow me to summon Asmodi and Gillamon.' You would then summon Asmodi and say, 'Asmodi, I ask that you allow me to summon Gillamon.' You would then summon Gillamon, and make your request directly to Gillamon. This process is the same for all the Demon Servants of Asmodi that follow in this section.

Maggid

Under Asmodi

To find an emergency source of money.
Magick performed under pressure is prone to failure, but performing the ritual is better than relying on hope. When you need money to get out of a situation, or to take advantage of an opportunity, use this power. If a result can come, it should come quickly.

To encourage people to bestow gifts upon you.
You can use this ritual at any time, and it works in a general way to make people you know, and even strangers, more likely to help you out or give you something you want. If you have a specific desire, you can also name what you want and the person who could gift it to you.

Maggid is pronounced as MAG-ID. MAG as in MAGAZINE. ID as in DID.

First summon Lucifer. Then summon Asmodi. Proceed to summon Maggid.

The Pathworking of Maggid

New grass growing in a muddy field.
A young girl dressed in white dances at the foot of a dead tree.
Bird feathers and tiny bones shine in the moonlight.
A starless desert at night, the horizon glowing with distant red fires.

Gillamon

Under Asmodi

To make somebody trust everything you say.
Name the person you wish to affect, and they will trust what you say, despite the evidence. This is most powerful in a personal relationship but can also be used in business and legal situations.

To make a group of people believe you are worthy of attention and investment.
When you reach a stage where you are about to make a presentation or proposal of some nature, and you need to be heard by the potential investors, this ritual brings power. The demons will make those you name believe you are worth listening to and they will feel safe investing in your idea. You do not need to name each individual, but name the company or group in a way that makes sense to you. It works most effectively when you speak before the group, but can also work when submitting something to a group remotely. (You can use this on an individual investor but it is more powerful when used on a group.)

Gillamon is pronounced as GILL-AM-ON. GILL as in GILL (like the GILL of a fish.) AM as in AM. ON as in ON.

First summon Lucifer. Then summon Asmodi. Proceed to summon Gillamon.

The Pathworking of Gillamon

Calm ocean waters at sunrise.
A thousand fish skeletons on the sandy beach.
In the sand dunes a black obelisk marked with veins of silver.

Ybarion

Under Asmodi

Make something ordinary appear special and desirable.
If you are selling something that is ordinary, you can make it appear rare, unique and special with this power, and this applies from something as small as an engagement ring to a house or business. The power can also be used when you bestow gifts that are not particularly special so that the recipient perceives them as far more valuable than they are. Describe your exact desire to the demon. This works more effectively if you know the name of the individual you are trying to convince, but if you are auctioning a house to a group of strangers you need only tell the demon to make the house appear as desirable as possible.

Make somebody think they are more talented than they are.
A large ego is an impediment to competitive progress. Make somebody think they are talented and they stop trying to learn and improve, which gives you the ability to get ahead of them.

Ybarion is pronounced as EE-BA-REE-ON. EE as in SEE. BA as in BAD. REE as in REED. ON as in ON.

First summon Lucifer. Then summon Asmodi. Proceed to summon Ybarion.

The Pathworking of Ybarion

Where two rivers meet, they turn the colour of mud.
The body of a wild boar, still warm, without sign of injury.
A four-way crossroads in the forest, with rain behind you and sunlight ahead.

Bakaron

Under Asmodi

Make an enemy's business fail.
A business is supported by many structures, but most of these are conceptual, held within the minds of those who work in the business. This power breaks those structures so that all who support the business become uncoordinated and unable to bring their skills to the business. It is rare for a business to fail overnight so do not expect immediate results. This power can be used against a competitor who is damaging your own business, or against any enemy that deserves the punishment. I will say that many people who fail in business experience relief, because the pressure is removed from their life, so if you seek to punish, you can ask the demon to bring chaos to the business, not complete failure.

To cause mistrust within any relationship.
Name two individuals, and you will cause mistrust between them with this power.

Bakaron is pronounced as BACK-ARE-ON. BACK as in BACK. ARE as in ARE. ON as in ON.

First summon Lucifer. Then summon Asmodi. Proceed to summon Bakaron.

The Pathworking of Bakaron

A field of poppies with snowy mountains in the distance.
A willow tree by a shallow river.
Halfway up a mountain, above the tree line, snow and rocks.

Presfees

Under Asmodi

To make somebody suffer in the way they made you suffer.
This is one of the finest revenge rituals because it will bring the experience of suffering to the one who hurt you. They will feel the same sensations that you experienced, even though they will be made to feel them through entirely different circumstances. It can take some months for this ritual to take full effect, but it brings great satisfaction.

To cause a person to act recklessly.
Be wary of any person to whom you apply this power, and do not be around them when there is the potential for danger. You would not, for example, get in a car with this person should they be driving. The purpose of this power is to make somebody reckless to the point where they make a mistake that damages their life, perhaps through poor decisions and actions at work, or by bringing an accident upon themselves.

Presfees is pronounced as PRES-FEAS. PRES as in PRESENT (with the S sounding like Z.) FEAS as in FEAST, so the name ends with the S sound.

First summon Lucifer. Then summon Asmodi. Proceed to summon Presfees.

The Pathworking of Presfees

A field of golden wheat.
The moon behind rainclouds.
A wheat field after a storm, flattened and rotting.
At the base of a mountain a wide outcrop of flat rock.

Hyla

Under Asmodi

To make a person doubt a plan.
A strategic power, this can be used to make anybody doubt a plan, whether it is their plan or that of another. There are countless situations where this can make it easier for you to put forward another plan or undermine somebody else.

Make somebody forgetful.
This power makes a named person generally forgetful, which makes them less effective in most situations. It will not make them forget something specific but is used to make them less able to deal with daily life.

Hyla is pronounced as HE-LA. HE as in HE. LA as in LARGE.

First summon Lucifer. Then summon Asmodi. Proceed to summon Hyla.

The Pathworking of Hyla

A grassy hilltop in blue morning twilight.
A smashed pomegranate mixed with human blood.
A rocky hilltop blazing with heat from the overhead sun.

Ormion

Under Asmodi

Cause people to remember what they like about you.
In any relationship, including those that are largely about business, you can gain an advantage, or the ability to progress, if you remind people that they like you. People who have seemingly forgotten or neglected you may see you as more important or worthy of promotion and respect. Name the individual that you wish to affect. This power does not work on groups of people.

Become less visible.
This power can make you less visible to specific people that you want to avoid. It can also make you less visible only to specific, named people. Or it can make you less visible in relation to a particular problem, such as a legal situation. Make your intention as clear as possible to the demon when making your request.

Ormion is pronounced as OAR-ME-ON. OAR as in BOAR. ME as in ME. ON as in ON.

First summon Lucifer. Then summon Asmodi. Proceed to summon Ormion.

The Pathworking of Ormion

In the middle of a field, reeds surround a pond.
The scattered bones of a human hand, yellow, soiled and as soft as chalk, scattered on dried earth.
Honey leaks from the remains of a broken iron jar.
In a long grassy valley, between hills and mountains, with a storm at one end of the valley and bright sunshine at the other.

The Demon Servants of Oriens

To summon the Demon Servants of Oriens, you must first summon Lucifer and ask Lucifer to grant you the power to summon the named Demon Duke and the Demon Servant.

If you were summoning Gagarin, you might say, 'Lucifer, I ask that you allow me to summon Oriens and Gagarin.' You would then summon Oriens and say, 'Oriens, I ask that you allow me to summon Gagarin.' You would then summon Gagarin, and make your request directly to Gagarin. This process is the same for all the Demon Servants of Oriens that follow in this section.

Gagarin

Under Oriens

To obtain approval or agreement from financial superiors.
This can help with getting a loan approval from a bank or any other agreement where you need somebody in power to agree to your financial suggestions and requests.

To get the best deal when buying or selling.
This power will help you get the best deal when selling a car, house or any item. Although it will give you an advantage in negotiations, do not assume it means you can ask for anything. Trust the magick but do not push it so far that you break the deal.

Gagarin is pronounced as GAG-ARE-IN. GAG as in GAG. ARE as in ARE. IN as in IN.

First summon Lucifer. Then summon Oriens. Proceed to summon Gagarin.

The Pathworking of Gagarin

A cave lit by a blue flame over a pool of black oil.
An old, naked woman, her hair sticky with dried blood.
In the centre of the cave, a silver chalice shines on a plinth of black rock.

Sarsiel

Under Oriens

To enable a never-ending cycle of misfortune.
This is a harsh curse that can have much more devastating
effects than you will see at the outset. Its purpose is to bring a
series of minor misfortunes that culminate into a crisis. A series
of speeding tickets, unexpected bills, and illnesses, the loss of a
job, a misunderstanding with a friend or problems at work, will
all combine to make life feel unbearable. The only weakness of
this ritual is that it can make even a skeptical person suspect
that they are cursed, and they may then seek to use protection
magick, which will, in some cases, bring them peace. It works
over many months, but you can expect to see some strain in the
early days. You can summon the demon and ask for the curse
to end should you feel that you have accomplished all that you
need.

**Bring disease that causes scars, blemishes and other forms of
ugliness.**
This is a form of revenge magick where you bring illness or
accident that makes a person uglier. In some cases, there is only
rapid aging or weight gain.

Sarsiel is pronounced as SAR-SEE-ALE. SAR as in SARCASM.
SEE as in SEE. ALE as in PALE.

First summon Lucifer. Then summon Oriens. Proceed to
summon Sarsiel.

The Pathworking of Sarsiel

A black tower on a hillside.
Hailstones fall in the bright green grass.
A man kneels, and arrow lodged in the back of his neck.
At the base of the tower, heat comes from its black bricks.

Sorosoma

Under Oriens

To expose somebody's secrets or cause them to be apprehended for their crimes.
When you know somebody is hiding something or has committed a crime, this ritual enables you to sit back and watch the drama unfold without any further effort. During the ritual, name the person and what you suspect, but ask that all their secrets be exposed, or that all their crimes come to light.

To cause those who deceive you to contract an illness.
This is not a ritual you aim at a specific person but is protective. If you believe there are those who deceive you in a harmful way, perform this ritual, and anybody who deceives you will become ill. It is normal for people to lie within a relationship, but this ritual will not cause your partner to become sick due to daily minor deceptions. If, however, your partner is deceiving you in a major way, they will become repeatedly unwell, which can be useful information.

Sorosoma is pronounced as SAW-ROW-SEW-MA. SAW as in SAW. ROW as in 'to ROW a boat'. SEW as in SEWING. MA as in MAGNET.

First summon Lucifer. Then summon Oriens. Proceed to summon Sorosoma.

The Pathworking of Sorosoma

A garden filled with white roses.
On loamy soil the transparent wings of a butterfly.
A hedge of thorns at the edge of the garden.

Zagal

Under Oriens

To bring sickness of the bowels.
A power like this can manifest with dramatic consequences or may only cause discomfort. It may cause stomach pain, constipation, or diarrhea. Direct it at a named individual.

To cause insomnia and nightmares.
This power can be used as punishment or to make another person weak when you need them to be. When you perform this ritual, know that the effect will be ongoing, often worsening over the months, until you summon Zagal once more, and ask that the named person no longer suffers. It may take some time for them to recover normal sleep habits.

Zagal is pronounced as ZAG-AL. ZAG as in ZIG-ZAG. AL as in BALANCE.

First summon Lucifer. Then summon Oriens. Proceed to summon Zagal.

The Pathworking of Zagal

A green, spring forest shimmers in a strong breeze.
The grass is grey and white.
On a brick-red stone, maggots drip from the remains of a rat.
The forest is still and moonlight shines through the leafless branches.

Turitil

Under Oriens

Cause somebody to experience panic and anxiety.
This power can be used to make somebody more vulnerable to episodes of anxiety and panic, or it can be directed at making them anxious during an upcoming situation. Ongoing anxiety can wreck a life so if you choose to reverse it, summon the demon once more and ask that the magick ends. This will not end the anxiety itself (as that will require the effort of the person you have harmed) but it will prevent the magick from continuing to have an effect.

To make somebody feel like a fraud.
An excellent way to defeat somebody is to make them doubt that they and their work have any value. If you wish an enemy or competitor to lose momentum, or even give up their work, use this power. It should always cause some pain and damaging doubt.

Turitil is pronounced as TOO-REE-TEAL. TOO as in TOO. REE as in REED. TEAL as in TEAL (rhymes with REAL).

First summon Lucifer. Then summon Oriens. Proceed to summon Turitil.

The Pathworking of Turitil

Flames rise from a rock on the beach, at night.
In the morning sky, the stars are smaller but brighter than ever.
A tree broken by lightning bleeds amber sap.

The Demon Servants of Ariton

To summon the Demon Servants of Ariton, you must first summon Lucifer and ask Lucifer to grant you the power to summon the named Demon Duke and Demon Servant.

If you were summoning Nilion, you might say, 'Lucifer, I ask that you allow me to summon Ariton and Nilion.' You would then summon Ariton and say, 'Ariton, I ask that you allow me to summon Nilion.' You would then summon Nilion, and make your request directly to Nilion. This process is the same for all the Demon Servants of Ariton that follow in this section.

Nilion

Under Ariton

To quieten noisy people, including neighbours.
There is another ritual that brings peace to an area, which can be used to quieten neighbours, but it works by reducing arguments and animosity. This power works only to reduce the amount of noise that people make. It will urge them to seek silence so that you can enjoy quieter times. If you do not know their names, name them in a way that makes sense to you.

Create harmony in a workplace you manage.
Harmony is not always a good thing, because it can make people complacent and lazy, but if you want harmony for a few months, this ritual can bring a coordinated peace to a workplace where you are in charge.

Nilion is pronounced as NIL-EE-AWN. NIL as in NIL. EE as in SEE. AWN as in FAWN.

First summon Lucifer. Then summon Ariton. Proceed to summon Nilion.

The Pathworking of Nilion

A rocky hilltop surrounded by mountains.
Snow falling on wet, black rock, where it melts.
A cliff wall dripping with fresh blood.

Maranaton

Under Ariton

To cause somebody to feel submissive in your presence.
Although this can be used in personal relationships, it is most often used to make somebody who is troublesome or somebody who has power over you, become more submissive. This gives you the potential to make many gains.

Make your partner more loving.
This is not a power of seduction or lust, but one of love. If there is no love within the person you name, there will be no effect, but if that love is hidden beneath distraction or resentment, it will be renewed.

Maranaton is pronounced as MARA-NA-TON. MARA as in MARATHON. NA as in NAP. TON as in BATON.

First summon Lucifer. Then summon Ariton. Proceed to summon Maranaton.

The Pathworking of Maranaton

From a mountaintop there is only cloud below, and hazy white sky above.
A white foam of rushing river through chalky rocks.
Ash and white blossom drift on the grey rock.
A desert of salt glaring white from the sun overhead.

Calamosi

Under Ariton

Overcome thoughts that torment you.
Effective for removing obsessive thoughts, especially when they arise from guilt or unfounded fear. When troubled by thoughts that repeatedly disturb you, whatever their source, you can ask Calamosi to bring relief and let those thoughts evaporate. This can bring great peace and free your mind for more important tasks or relaxation.

Bring justice to those who have worked against you.
The power works against thieves who have not yet been apprehended, friends who have betrayed, individuals who have worked against your business, and direct enemies. During the ritual, ask Calamosi to bring justice to anybody you perceive to have worked against you. The justice meted out will be severe although it may take time to transpire.

Calamosi is pronounced as CAL-AM-OWE-SEE. CAL as in CALCULATE. AM as in AM. OWE as in OWE. SEE as in SEE.

First summon Lucifer. Then summon Ariton. Proceed to summon Calamosi.

The Pathworking of Calamosi

The scorched remains of a forest at dawn.
Smoke leaking from a broken rock.
A breeze that smells of raw fish, salt and seaweed.
A lone tree in an endless meadow.

Rosaran

Under Ariton

To bring fortune in a legal situation.
In some legal situations, you need luck, otherwise known as fortune. This ritual can increase your chances of having things go your way, even when you are in the wrong.

To let others see the deception in a fraud.
If ever you want to cause gurus, managers, and other authority figures to lose the respect of those that follow them, use this ritual. You do not even need to know the real name of the person, only the name they are known by. If the person is genuine it will have no effect, but if they are deceptive (as most gurus are, for example), the veil will drop, and their followers will see them as the frauds they are.

Rosaran is pronounced as ROSE-ARE-RAN. ROSE as in ROSE. ARE as in ARE. RAN as in RAN.

First summon Lucifer. Then summon Ariton. Proceed to summon Rosaran.

The Pathworking of Rosaran

At sunset, a noose hangs from a rotting tree.
The skeletons of birds in rotten black leaves.
In the rain, the remains of a bonfire.
At the edge of the musty forest, a glimpse of distant black mountains.

Semeot

Under Ariton

Overcome nerves and anxiety in high-pressure situations.
For those who speak in public or make presentations, this is an obvious choice, but it can also be effective for those who perform in competitive sports, or soldiers entering battle. It should only be used if you know nerves and anxiety are a problem for you. The ritual will increase your ability to find calm when the pressure begins to increase.

Discover new ways of working.
Whatever your profession, or whatever personal skill or craft you indulge in, working in the same way is reliable but stifling. Discover new ways of working, and you can become more effective and competitive.

Semeot is pronounced as SEMI-OT. SEMI as in SEMICOLON. OT as in HOT.

First summon Lucifer. Then summon Ariton. Proceed to summon Semeot.

The Pathworking of Semeot

Moonlight on a frosted field.
A red sunrise through the pale, misty sky.
Standing in the shadow of enormous rock, the glare of sunshine over the wheat fields.

The Demon Servants of Magoth

To summon the Demon Servants of Magoth, you must first summon Lucifer and ask Lucifer to grant you the power to summon the named Demon Duke and Demon Servant.

If you were summoning Corocon, you might say, 'Lucifer, I ask that you allow me to summon Magoth and Corocon.' You would then summon Magoth and say, 'Magoth, I ask that you allow me to summon Corocon.' You would then summon Corocon, and make your request directly to Corocon. This process is the same for all the Demon Servants of Magoth that follow in this section.

Tagora

Under Magoth

Compel somebody to pay what they owe.
Bad debtors will feel a compulsion to pay. Remind the person who owes you, in a manner that feels right to you, a day after performing the ritual. If they still refuse, apply a curse of some kind, and that can bring more weakness, giving this power a chance to take full effect.

Cause a competitor to believe they have done all that can be done.
Later in the book, there is a power to make an enemy believe they have won, thus making them weaker. This power is less about enemies, but about preparing for competition. If you are about to enter a chess tournament, you can make your opponent believe nothing more needs to be done, giving you the advantage. In games and business, this can be an excellent power that leaves you more prepared than a named competitor. If there are several competitors, name them all.

Tagora is pronounced as TAG-ORA. TAG as in TAG. ORA as in ORAL.

First summon Lucifer. Then summon Magoth. Proceed to summon Tagora.

The Pathworking of Tagora

A hammer of iron on a pebbled beach.
Lightning from a blue sky, over the ocean.
Wet footprints on pale grey rock.
Five barren trees in a field of grass, their bark made black by torrential rain.

Corocon

Under Magoth

To bring relief from pain.
This ritual is designed to bring relief to chronic pain conditions. Often, there is an immediate lessening of the pain, but sometimes you find it takes some days before you notice an improvement in the condition. In no way a cure, this is a useful way to cope with conditions that refuse to improve.

To encourage fertility.
This will not make you fertile if you are sterile, but when seeking to become pregnant, it increases your chances, all other things being equal. The ritual can be carried out by either partner or by both. It does not require the knowledge of the other, should you choose to perform it in secret. This is a personal power and will not work on other people, such as friends and relatives.

Corocon is pronounced as CORE-AWE-CORN. CORE as in CORE. AWE as in AWE. CORN as in CORN.

First summon Lucifer. Then summon Magoth. Proceed to summon Corocon.

The Pathworking of Corocon

Three rusted daggers in the snow.
Frost on red Rowan berries.
A quiet stream trickles through the morning forest.

Dulid

Under Magoth

To heal injury and sickness in an animal.
I believe this power would have been used for livestock, not pets, and it can indeed be used by farmers. For those with pets, the magick can be directed at the animal you care about, and it increases the chance and speed of recovery.

To endure pain with bravery until healing occurs.
Any occult text that promises complete protection from injury is a deception, so if you find yourself with a broken leg, or enduring any painful therapy required for recovery, use this ritual to find bravery. That bravery makes the experience less painful and easier to endure. You can direct the ritual at somebody else who is suffering if you know them personally, and you do not need to tell them about the magick.

Dulid is pronounced as DULL-EED. DULL as in DULL. EED as in SEED.

First summon Lucifer. Then summon Magoth. Proceed to summon Dulid.

The Pathworking of Dulid

The horns of a ram on a slab of granite.
An apple tree overladen with fruit.
A wheat field after a storm, flattened and rotting.
A grassy hilltop overlooking the smoking remains of a burnt forest.

Arakison

Under Magoth

To break an addiction.

You can direct this power at another person, but it will only work if they are trying to beat the addiction. If you are suffering from an addiction, the power will support your efforts to beat the addiction, helping you endure the worst withdrawals, side-effects, and cravings. Withdrawing from any addiction can be dangerous, so don't think magick takes those dangers away. Break an addiction with professional support, but give yourself an advantage through the power of Arakison.

To limit the effects of disease and illness.

This power can be used on yourself or somebody you know, and will prevent an illness from following its most intense path. It is not a cure but makes recovery quicker, or progress of disease slower. It does not replace medical help but makes the help you get more effective.

Arakison is pronounced as ARACK-EE-SON. ARACK as in BARACK. EE as in SEE. SON as in SONNET.

First summon Lucifer. Then summon Magoth. Proceed to summon Arakison.

The Pathworking of Arakison

Rotten reeds at the edge of a frozen lake.
A four-way crossroads, each pathway made from crushed charcoal.
A dead tree in the middle of a ploughed field.

Daglus

Under Magoth

To cause one you desire to feel passion for you.
If you feel an authentic desire for somebody, this power can make that person feel passion for you. Even if they dislike you intellectually, the sexual tension will arise. Seduction magick of any kind is subject to many factors, and those include your ability to recognise and act upon any change at the right time. Hone your perception and be confident. Even if somebody feels passion, they may refuse to act on it, so this isn't a pass that allows you to force yourself on somebody. It is a powerful way to give you the best chance to make a person weak with desire.

To make a disinterested lover passionate.
In a relationship, should your lover lose interest in you, this power can arouse sexual desire once more.

Daglus is pronounced as DAY-GLUES. DAY as in DAY. GLUES as in GLUES.

First summon Lucifer. Then summon Magoth. Proceed to summon Daglus.

The Pathworking of Daglus

Grey clouds over a lake of blood at dawn.
A fallen tree in an empty field, the full moon in blue sky.
Red leaves coat the ground of a treeless grassland.

The Demon Servants of Beelzebub

To summon the Demon Servants of Beelzebub, you must first summon Lucifer and ask Lucifer to grant you the power to summon the named Demon Duke and Demon Servant.

If you were summoning Bilek, you might say, 'Lucifer, I ask that you allow me to summon Beelzebub and Bilek.' You would then summon Beelzebub and say, 'Beelzebub, I ask that you allow me to summon Bilek.' You would then summon Bilek, and make your request directly to Bilek. This process is the same for all the Demon Servants of Beelzebub that follow in this section.

Diralisin

Under Beelzebub

To open communication.
Even when the doors appear to be closed, and communication seems impossible, you can make a named person far more willing to talk to you. This works in damaged relationships, but also when you are trying to get somebody in a business or organisation to listen to your ideas.

Make an enemy believe they have already won.
One of the easiest ways to defeat an enemy is to give them more confidence than they deserve. When you name an enemy, Diralisin will make that enemy believe they have defeated you. Whether this is in a personal or business situation, or even in other forms of competition, this belief will weaken your opponent and give you the opportunity to advance.

Diralisin is pronounced as DEER-AL-ISS-IN. DEER as in DEER. AL as in BALANCE. ISS as in HISS. IN as in IN.

First summon Lucifer. Then summon Beelzebub. Proceed to summon Diralisin.

The Pathworking of Diralisin

A meadow of grass and flowers, and on the horizon a forest in flames.
Scorched human hair on a freshly dug grave.
A leafless tree by the edge of a lake, where the wind is harsh and cold.

Camalon

Under Beelzebub

To compel a person to leave their home, workplace, or any other position.
This ritual can make somebody move out of their home overnight, but often it takes longer for somebody to get organised, so in most cases, it will set the wheels in motion. If the person refuses to move, do not repeat this, but after some weeks, use other rituals to cause fear and anxiety, or other discomforts that may make them wish to move. If you want somebody to leave a workplace or any other position where they are affecting you negatively, this can also cause them to leave.

To cause one person to be violent to another.
You may wish to create a violent argument, or worse, to ruin a reputation, bring harm, or improve your position in a given situation. Be cautious when you are around those named in the ritual.

Camalon is pronounced as CAM-AL-ON. CAM as in CAMERA. AL as in BALANCE. ON as in ON.

First summon Lucifer. Then summon Beelzebub. Proceed to summon Camalon.

The Pathworking of Camalon

The first light of morning brightens a freezing cave.
Outside, light so bright you cannot see anything but white.
A crescent moon in the morning sky.
A quiet place in the cool forest, with five standing stones.

Bilek

Under Beelzebub

Cause somebody to change their mind or reverse a decision.
When somebody has made up their mind or made a decision that goes against your wishes, it often feels like there is nothing more to be done. Using this ritual, you stand more chance of getting a named person, a group of people, or even an organisation to reverse a decision.

To make those who work for you respectful and obedient.
Should you be in a position where others work for you, and this even applies to online virtual assistants and other remote appointments, you can make your employees respectful and obedient. This ensures they will work hard for you. It doesn't guarantee they will be trustworthy, but it lessens the chance of them stealing or betraying you in any way. You can name specific people, or if you work in a large company, ask for all your employees to be affected.

Bilek is pronounced as BEE-LEC. BEE as in BEE. LEC as in LECTURE.

First summon Lucifer. Then summon Beelzebub. Proceed to summon Bilek.

The Pathworking of Bilek

Sandy desert dunes at dawn.
A pale man with three bleeding cuts on his cheeks.
A broken arrow lies in the sand.
A pool of filthy water surrounded by sand.

Corilon

Under Beelzebub

To crush the ambitions of somebody who wishes to defeat you in a legal argument.
Even the humblest people find themselves embroiled in legal situations, such as when a family member unfairly contests a will. This power will crush the ambition of that person. Name them in the ritual, and Corilon will take away their ambition, The legal proceedings will either be brought to a halt or will proceed with such a lack of energy that you will win.

To improve a skill in a short period of time.
When you commit to improving a skill during a period of time that is less than six months, Corilon will vastly increase the ability with which you learn. It can be used for hobbies but is incredibly powerful when used by those training for a new job or position. If you are attempting to pass an exam, it will not help with the exam itself, but can improve your learning skills.

Corilon is pronounced as CORE-EE-LON. CORE as in CORE. EE as in SEE. LON as in LONG.

First summon Lucifer. Then summon Beelzebub. Proceed to summon Corilon.

The Pathworking of Corilon

An emerald lake surrounded by mountains.
The body of a dead snake, its eyes white.
You stand at the edge of a fast and foaming river in the moonlight.

Borob

Under Beelzebub

To improve lucid dreams and astral experiences.
For those who are working on the experience of astral projection and lucid dreaming, Borob can increase your ability to have this experience.

Create a veil over an object or place, so nobody looks there.
To hide a physical object, you ask Borob to cast a veil over the place where it is hidden. In the simplest terms, let us imagine that you have hidden a most valued page of secrets inside a book on your shelf. Casting a veil over this means nobody will have any interest in this book. You can also hide entire attics, cellars, rooms and other spaces where you wish to conceal physical objects.

Borob is pronounced as BAW-ROB. BAW as in BAWL. ROB as in ROBIN.

First summon Lucifer. Then summon Beelzebub. Proceed to summon Borob.

The Pathworking of Borob

A fallow field, hard with winter frost.
At twilight, three bright stars above the horizon.
A human spine, ancient, brown, broken in two.
The edge of a grassy cliff, overlooking the moonlit ocean.

Gramon

Under Beelzebub

To create an air of dignity.
The ability to appear dignified is utterly lacking in those who are filled with self-doubt, or those who have developed their personality in a state of oppression. Dignity is an underestimated power, and when you appear dignified, you command attention, respect, and trust. You become much more attractive to others. The power of Gramon will bring an air of dignity that will grow slowly over the coming months.

Attract fame through magickal glamour.
If you are working on finding fame (and you must be working on this in some way because nothing will come from nothing), Gramon can assist. A magickal glamour is an illusion or forced perception. There are many kinds of glamour, often used to make people more attractive. This glamour will make you appear worthier of the obsessive fascination that leads to fame. Without a platform on which to be seen, it will have no effect.

Gramon is pronounced as GRAM-ON. GRAM as in GRAM. ON as in ON.

First summon Lucifer. Then summon Beelzebub. Proceed to summon Gramon.

The Pathworking of Gramon

Beyond the meadows, snowy mountains at dawn.
Wheat trampled underfoot.
The bones of a bird coated with human vomit.
Burned tree stumps surrounded by embers and ashes.

The Demon Servants of Paymon

To summon the Demon Servants of Paymon, you must first summon Lucifer and ask Lucifer to grant you the power to summon the named Demon Duke and Demon Servant.

If you were summoning Ebaron, you might say, 'Lucifer, I ask that you allow me to summon Paymon and Ebaron.' You would then summon Paymon and say, 'Paymon, I ask that you allow me to summon Ebaron.' You would then summon Ebaron, and make your request directly to Ebaron. This process is the same for all the Demon Servants of Paymon that follow in this section.

Sumuron

Under Paymon

To discover gifts and abilities.

When you are feeling uninspired or if you need to find a new direction in work, or for personal entertainment, knowing your gifts and natural abilities is essential. To discover you can paint like a master at the age of sixty is a minor tragedy. Discover what you can about yourself, being open to the words of the demon during the ritual, and feelings and jolts of intuition in the following weeks.

Find inspiration for creative projects.

This power works more for the arts than for projects such as marketing or business. If you need artistic creativity, this ritual can bring a rapid development in your ability to find inspiration.

Sumuron is pronounced as SUM-OOR-ON. SUM as in SUMMER. OOR as in POOR. ON as in ON.

First summon Lucifer. Then summon Paymon. Proceed to summon Sumuron.

The Pathworking of Sumuron

A misty valley strewn with broken rocks.
A silver spear, its tip coated in gore.
The full moon rises red over black mountains.

Ebaron

Under Paymon

Sense what the future holds.
When you feel the need to know what is coming up in your life, call on Ebaron to tell you what you most need to know. Do not name a specific situation unless you are desperate to know how that situation will develop. You will often obtain answers and images during the ritual, but other thoughts will occur to you in the following days. Give yourself some time where you are quiet and alone, or out walking, so that such thoughts and images have the space to be noticed. If you stare at your phone all day, you won't have the room to sense anything beyond the ordinary.

To find that which is lost.
A simple power to recover an item of any kind that has been lost or stolen.

Ebaron is pronounced as EBB-ARE-ON. EBB as in EBB. ARE as in ARE. ON as in ON.

First summon Lucifer. Then summon Paymon. Proceed to summon Ebaron.

The Pathworking of Ebaron

A flooded field, water stretching to the horizon.
A bonfire atop a hill.
The claw marks of birds on a cliff face.
Standing at the edge of a lake of blood.

Zalomes

Under Paymon

To uncover secrets that affect you.
When you suspect that secrets are being used against you, at work or in your personal life, ask Zalomes to reveal any secrets that may be harming or limiting your progress in life. What you find may be concrete evidence or an intuitive perception, but it will be enough to give you a strategic advantage.

To outwit those who steal your ideas.
If you own any intellectual property, and others seek to steal it, usurp it or create derivative works based on your concepts, this power enables you to outwit and defeat your competitor in the ensuing battle.

Zalomes is pronounced as ZA-LOAM-EZZ. ZA as in ZAP. LOAM as in LOAM. EZZ as in FEZZ.

First summon Lucifer. Then summon Paymon. Proceed to summon Zalomes.

The Pathworking of Zalomes

A black horse galloping on the horizon.
A motionless man in flames, feeling no pain.
Saplings grow through the marshy grass.

Takaros

Under Paymon

To make a lover faithful.
Whether or not you suspect a lover, this ritual can bring peace of mind, ensuring that your partner's attention remains only on you.

Force somebody to reveal secrets they planned to keep.
Knowing when to use this is the most difficult part of the process, because if somebody has a secret, you may not know. If, however, you suspect that somebody is keeping something from you, ask Takaros to compel that person to reveal the secret. Many people will spontaneously confess to their misdemeanours in the days or weeks that follow.

Takaros is pronounced as TACK-ARE-OZ. TACK as in TACK. ARE as in ARE. OZ as in OZ (think of *The Wizard of...*)

First summon Lucifer. Then summon Paymon. Proceed to summon Takaros.

The Pathworking of Takaros

Dead birds rotting in a sunlit forest.
A polished black stone on a plinth of gold.
A flat sandstone rock in a forest glade.

Zugola

Under Paymon

To win competitions by influencing judges.

If you know the names of the judges, name them. If not, name the competition you wish to win, and state the nature of the entry. Tell the demon whether you are competing in a football match or have submitted a painting to an art competition. This power works for individual events that take place on one day, not entire championships or long competitions, so if the work is ongoing, this is a ritual that may require frequent repetition.

To quell an argument and bring peace.

This can be used to bring peace when you are stuck in an argument with another, or it can be directed a people you know who are arguing. Useful during divorce and other situations where tempers flare. It can even be used to make people who live near to you less argumentative, bringing peace to the area. The power can also be directed at personal and family arguments that continually arise. It will lay them to rest.

Zugola is pronounced as ZOO-GORE-LA. ZOO as in ZOO. GORE as in GORE. LA as in LAP.

First summon Lucifer. Then summon Paymon. Proceed to summon Zugola.

The Pathworking of Zugola

A white river between black mountains.
A pale child carries a rusted dagger.
A pebbled beach by an ocean as still and black as a lake.

The Demon Servants of Amaymon

To summon the Demon Servants of Amaymon, you must first summon Lucifer and ask Lucifer to grant you the power to summon the named Demon Duke and Demon Servant.

If you were summoning Akorok, you might say, 'Lucifer, I ask that you allow me to summon Amaymon and Akorok.' You would then summon Amaymon and say, 'Amaymon, I ask that you allow me to summon Akorok.' You would then summon Akorok, and make your request directly to Akorok. This process is the same for all the Demon Servants of Amaymon that follow in this section.

Akorok

Under Amaymon

Make somebody unable to perform magick clearly.
If you know somebody who performs magick, name them, and they will stumble over words, make mistakes, and lose concentration, weakening their magick.

To remove traces of yourself from a home.
When leaving a home to move to a new one, you may wish to remove any impressions you have left behind. Although it is rare, there are some individuals whose personal evil and anger can infect you by connecting to your recent presence. This is a safeguard against accidental infection such as that, but also prevents anybody with psychic abilities from sensing anything about you.

Akorok is pronounced as ACK-OR-OCK. ACK as in BACK. OR as in OR. OCK as in ROCK.

First summon Lucifer. Then summon Amaymon. Proceed to summon Akorok.

The Pathworking of Akorok

Hail stones from a black night sky.
A frozen lake, smeared with bloody handprints.
A three-forked crossroads, scattered with human teeth.

Dalep

Under Amaymon

Discover the most peaceful solution.
There are many ways to attack, get revenge and find satisfaction, but if you seek the most peaceful solution to a difficult situation, summon Dalep and ask for guidance.

To break out of current patterns.
If you are habitually thinking the same thoughts, acting in the same way, and becoming stale in your life and personality, ask Dalep to help you break free from these patterns and discover new potential.

Dalep is pronounced as DAR-LEP. DAR as in DARK. LEP as in LEPROSY.

First summon Lucifer. Then summon Amaymon. Proceed to summon Dalep.

The Pathworking of Dalep

An old man in filthy robes points at the sun.
A crescent moon in the sunset.
Two children kneel before a standing stone.
A sapling in flames without being consumed by the fire.

Bariol

Under Amaymon

Improve your willpower.
Summon Bariol and ask for your willpower to increase. This increase in willpower can be general but is especially useful for making difficult projects feel easier. It helps you to complete projects that would otherwise go unfinished.

Bariol is pronounced as BARRY-OLL. BARRY is like MARRY starting with B rather than M. OLL as in DOLL.

Embrace the power of patience.
Action can be less effective than patience, but when you need patience the most it is almost impossible to achieve. Summon Bariol and ask for patience when you need it to survive a specific situation.

First summon Lucifer. Then summon Amaymon. Proceed to summon Bariol.

The Pathworking of Bariol

A barren land of dry earth.
An old man with an erect phallus.
Wine poured over human faeces.
A dark and musty cave where it is difficult to breathe.

Cargosik

Under Amaymon

Make an enemy feel sympathy for you.
Until a few years ago this was one of the best-kept secrets of the hidden Orders, but it has become widely known that if you make your enemy love you, or at least sympathise with you, there is no need to win. The war is over. Summon Cargosik to bring this feeling to your named enemy. You can let the war between you end or use this moment as an opportunity to attack and cause more damage than would otherwise be possible.

To clear and charm a new home.
When you move into a new home, perform this ritual as soon as you can, but after you have moved your personal possessions into place. It will ensure that unwanted traces of other people and spirits are banished and will bring an atmosphere of strength and warmth to the home.

Cargosik is pronounced as CARGO-SEEK. CARGO as in CARGO. SEEK as in SEEK.

First summon Lucifer. Then summon Amaymon. Proceed to summon Cargosik.

The Pathworking of Cargosik

A waterfall streaming with blood.
Worms boiling from the soil.
A circle of shattered human skulls.
A dried lake of salt, white as snow.

236

Nilima

Under Amaymon

Find balance between optimism and negativity.
An overly optimistic person is liable to make plans that cannot be achieved or sustained, while a negative person is too frozen to act. You may not be clear about where you are in terms of optimism and negativity, because it has been shown that people have false beliefs about this. The wise choice is to summon Nilima and ask for your personality to find balance between optimism and negativity. This can be done at any time, but if you are embarking on a new project or a change of life, it can be an essential step to take.

To find courage.
If you have never felt courageous, the power of Nilima will have a clear appeal. If you have lost courage, it can be regained. If you feel courage, but want more of it, Nilima will grant this. Courage is not recklessness, but the ability to see the dangers and problems, and face them with full integrity.

Nilima is pronounced as KNEE-LEE-MA. KNEE as in KNEE. LEE as in LEEK. MA as in MAP.

First summon Lucifer. Then summon Amaymon. Proceed to summon Nilima.

The Pathworking of Nilima

A field of rotten wheat.
The moon behind rainclouds.
Horse hoofprints in the clay.
A field of flowers at dawn.

Working with Lucifer

It is said that Lucifer grants the power to make a situation reach its conclusion more rapidly, by manipulating time. Used wisely, this power can achieve many of your aims. You can make somebody age internally or mentally, at a rapid rate. You can bring a future success into reality sooner. A relationship can flourish with passion in hours rather than weeks.

When you have worked with the powers of Lucifer, you will see that he fulfils requests with great force, and this can sometimes cause disruption with the effects of your magick rippling and resonating with many other situations. You should not see this as a problem, but as something you accept in making your request. It would be cowardly to assume that these disruptive effects are anything other than the natural and expected consequences of the request you have made. If you use magick to lure somebody into your life, or to end a business arrangement, or to cause great sickness, all these situations would bring disruption no matter what the timeline. The difference is that if you solved these problems without Lucifer's power, these disruptions and changes would occur as slowly as the solution. When you shift time and force events to occur more rapidly, it is logical to assume that the changes that go with the result will also rush into your life more rapidly.

Do not let the fear of change make you shun Lucifer, but you may be wise to make your first request one that will give you a gentle taste for the nature of this power.

If you work with the other demons in this book, and even if you have no intention of working with Lucifer directly, you will summon Lucifer so often (for he is called at the opening of each ritual), that you will gain a familiarity with the Demon King. You will feel at ease rather than in awe, although you may feel awe at his abilities. This is an important distinction. If you adore and worship Lucifer, your connection to him will lessen. Have you ever been in a relationship where somebody is so infatuated with you that they created fantasies and delusions about your gifts and qualities? This is usually an irritation. Unless you are a narcissist, you do not want to be worshiped, especially under false pretences. Lucifer does not seek worship, but partnership. The Demon King has respect for you, not power over you, and wishes to work with your desire to bring you a chosen reality. Do not fawn before him, but speak with strength, good manners, and honesty. Make your request, not humbly, but knowing that Lucifer wants to bring you satisfaction.

It was mentioned earlier that you only need to summon a demon once for any given problem, and this is true except when a situation is complex and ever-changing. For the more complex problems, you may turn to Lucifer, because he can adapt his powers to so many aspects of a problem or situation. If you choose to work with Lucifer, know that he has many powers that go beyond the one listed earlier in the book. It could be said that he has all the powers listed for every demon, and this would be no lie.

The other demons are Lucifer's Legion, and to reject them as unimportant is not pleasing to Lucifer. If one of the other demons in the book can solve your problem, work with that demon. Never assume that it is easier to work with Lucifer for every situation. With Lucifer, the speed and disruption will be greater. This is not always what you want.

Place great value on the powers and qualities of the Legion of Demons, but know that their powers can also be granted by Lucifer if you are willing to accept the consequences brought by disruptive change.

I will give no further warning, but I will say that if you summon Lucifer with the intention of using a power usually attributed to another demon, you may wish to seek his advice first. Ask if you will be satisfied by the result. If you sense no response from Lucifer, this may be due to lack of practice and ability. If that is the case, summon other demons until you strengthen your connection to Lucifer.

Conclusion

When you wish to perform magick with success, it is said that you should take heed *to know, to will, to dare, and to keep silent.*

To know, read about magick and understand the directions without excess haste, unburdened by previous beliefs.

To will, select the change you are going to make in reality and decide that it will be so.

To dare, perform the magick, knowing that it will work.

To keep silent, you speak to nobody of your active rituals until they work, and let doubts and fears remain unspoken.

A knowledgeable member of The Order put it more pithily when he said, 'Learn the rituals, know who you are and what you want, do the magick and stop talking about it.'

The Order of Unveiled Faces believes in the power, dignity, and importance of magick. Magick is a secret because it will remain unseen by those who stare at it directly. It will be sensed by those who are born to work with its wonders. For those who seek magick, we swear an oath to provide you only with the methods that we know to be true. We swear to advocate for the validity and significance of magick.

If you are new and confused, this book can give you what you want. If you know magick, this book can provide a new bearing. If you think you know everything already we can't change your mind, so we hope you get what you need from your current beliefs.

We are not a cult of believers who shun those who voice an alternate opinion. We are not the only way to discover Lucifer and the demons. Judge us on the quality of what we divulge, not on convention or dogmata. In magick, there is no room for the fanatic. For the willful and determined, with the intelligence to rebel against destiny, there a delicate opportunity known as potential, and that is where magick is to be found.

TR, AC, LC, LE, RM & AW

Further Reading

The Book of Abramelin: A New Translation - Revised and Expanded by George Dehn, Steven Guth and Abraham von Worms, 2015. ISBN: 9780892542147
The final sourcebook used to complete the work of our Order.

The Veritable Key of Solomon by Dr. Stephen Skinner, 2010. ISBN: 0955738768
There are useful details on the origins of Lucifer legends, myths, and sigils.

The Lesser Key of Solomon by Joseph H. Peterson, 1999. ISBN: 9781578632206
A work that enables you to see how easily magick can be corrupted.

Grimorium Verum by Joseph H. Peterson, 2007. ISBN: 1434811166
This is another work revealing original sources and their subsequent development. The magick itself is false, and the book is worthwhile only to understand the erroneous development and debasement of occultism.

43833182R00146

Printed in Poland
by Amazon Fulfillment
Poland Sp. z o.o., Wrocław